Seashells

OF THE

Caribbean

Lesley Sutty

CARIBBEAN

First published 1990

Published by MACMILLAN EDUCATION LTD
London and Basingstoke
*Associated companies and representatives in Accra,
Auckland, Delhi, Dublin, Gaborone, Hamburg, Harare,
Hong Kong, Kuala Lumpur, Lagos, Manzini, Melbourne,
Mexico City, Nairobi, New York, Singapore, Tokyo.*

ISBN 0-333-52191-9

Printed in Hong Kong

A CIP catalogue record for this book is available from
the British Library.

Contents

This book is dedicated to Kay Whiteside

Introduction

The Caribbean Sea stretches from the Gulf of Mexico to the Venezuelan Basin over a distance of more than 2500 miles; a mosaic of hundreds of luxuriant volcanic and coral islands, whose reefs and lagoons are home to more than 1200 molluscan species. The nature of the marine shell fauna of this region is extremely diverse; seeking shelter beneath the sand of beaches, under the rocks of coastal areas, in the soft deep mud of estuaries, in dark submarine caves, in the thick growths of marine prairies, and under branches of vast coral outcrops; it remains unobtrusive and often difficult to discover. Each species has its geographical distribution and populations vary in size, shape and colour according to environment; some animals migrate seasonally far afield. Tidal movement in the Caribbean is unspectacular other than during the Spring and Autumn equinoxes when shallow reefs and sand flats emerge briefly. The intertidal zone remains stable and undisturbed, with the exception of the passage of tropical storms and hurricanes, governing the lives of many gastropods and bi-valves.

Some of the world's rarest shells live in West Indian waters: the Golden Cowrie, the Leaf Winged Murex and the Glory of the Altantic Cone. The equally beautiful but common Pink Queen Conch and King Helmet shells are still abundant in shallow waters. Numerous miniature, finely sculptured shells are mixed with the fine sands of tidelines which act as a boundary between sea and shore.

The intention of this guide is to introduce amateurs and collectors to an intertidal and shallow water fauna which has aroused the curiosity of the thousands of visitors I have met over the years throughout our islands, and which represented for them the West Indies.

Many of the shells illustrated are amongst the most common and certainly exotic of the Caribbean. Many areas in the Greater and Lesser Antilles have been defined as Parks, where it is possible to become familiar with the animals that are the builders of an intricate and fascinating shell masonry.

Lesley Sutty

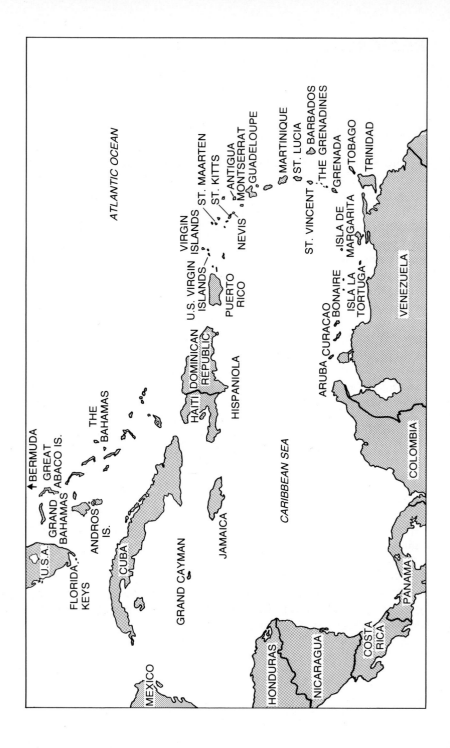

The molluscan animal

600 million years ago, the ocean's sediment, rich in bacterial growth, protozoans and abundant organic debris, accelerated the development of marine invertebrates, animals without backbones. A small shelled mollusc resembling a conical tent and housing a wormlike creature, appeared on the scene. It was a *monoplacophoran* or gastroverm, ancestor to the strange living fossil *Neopilina* which emerged from a depth of 2000 fathoms during dredging operations off the Pacific coast of Costa Rica in 1952. This was to be a major scientific discovery of the twentieth century whereby one of the most ancient members of the animal kingdom proved it had continued to exist in its original form through four geological eras. These early marine shell builders developed and diverged, creating a complexity of shapes, sizes and colours by secreting through their mantles a variety of nutrients absorbed from their oceanic environment.

The biological diversity of this fauna and its remarkable adaptability to countless adverse conditions, including alternating periods of glaciation and warming of the earth's crust, was to make them animals rich in information as to how life had evolved. The primitive, slow moving *polyplacophoran*, the articulated chiton, and the steamlined limpets, hung tenaciously with strong suction caps to coastal reefs, cliffs and shores, enjoying the constant renewal of oxygen and unaffected by the many tons of weight represented by the breaking of each wave. The sedentary oyster cemented itself to solid supports, feeding on and filtering the sea's planktonic resources. Scallops clapped their valves and swam through the water if danger menaced. Snails or gastropods, the prolific bottom dwellers, the benthic creatures, explored at length the vast ocean floor. The burrowing augers, turrets and olives moved through the sediment with only long sensory siphons showing. Ferocious *cephalopods*; squids, octopuses and nautili, were impressive, strong and untiring pelagic swimmers using sophisticated jet propulsion. A lesser member of the realm was to flout convention by discarding the weighty outer shell in order to swim and crawl freely; this was the *nudibranch*, the seaslug, who chose to expose its rare, exotic and beautiful mantle decorations to all. Far beyond the reach of man lived countless fragile, transparent molluscs, part of an abyssal fauna, 3000 fathoms below the ocean's surface. The mollusc colonised every part of the earth;

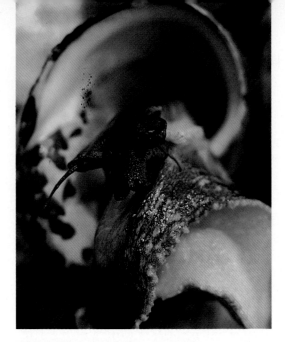

WEST INDIAN TOP SHELL, *Cittarium pica*

its lakes and rivers, mountains, forest and prairies, the seashore and the oceans.

Today molluscs outnumber all living vertebrates and are second in importance only to the insect phylum. More than 80,000 species of marine shells live in cold, temperate and tropical waters. Marine molluscs recently submitted to stringent cellular tests under laboratory conditions, and benefiting from the triple protection of a limy shell, a thick calcareous operculum, and their burrowing ability, proved conclusively that they would be the only members of the animal kingdom to survive total irradiation of our planet. Yet these fascinating shell carrying creatures, like so many others of the animal kingdom, face a hazardous future, as many of their long established habitats are destroyed with the development and construction of the world's coastal areas. Most now have only one chance in ten million of dying of old age.

Molluscan habitats

The littoral and intertidal zone

Four-fifths of the earth's flora and fauna lives on the edge of the world's oceans. The shore line, or littoral zone, is so called because of the many millions of *Littorina* snails that live there in pools, creeks or on sand flats, clinging to rocks and cliff faces; constantly exposed to wave action and an immense exchange of oxygen. It is a rich and fascinating area, where a great diversity of life abounds and molluscs find an unlimited supply of food, be they vegetarian or carnivore. Chitons, top shells and periwinkles have colonised our coasts in vast numbers. Beneath rocks large families of hermit crabs live in adopted homes, which are usually colourful cast-off shells of other seasnails. The tidelines are home to sand loving turrids and clams.

Just above these two zones is the splash zone, a predominantly dry area subjected to infrequent saltwater soakings from turbulent seas.

Estuaries

Molluscs living in the fluctuating saline conditions of estuaries are particularly hardy species and include clams, cones and crown conchs. Although recognised as important nurseries and breeding grounds for both shells and fish, rivers and estuaries are increasingly threatened by toxic waste and pollution, and are used as convenient sewers throughout the Caribbean. Shellfish collected from many such areas are known to contain levels of toxins and bacteria dangerous to both humans and seabirds.

The mangrove swamp

The tidal mudflats so common in temperate zones exist in the Caribbean, but generally remain submerged due to minimal tide movement. In the West Indies these areas are more closely associated with the mangrove swamps, which have colonised many thousands of miles of tropical and sub-tropical coastlines. The submerged roots of the mangrove trees form an impenetrable, inundated forest, and an ecosystem rich in organic sediment which favours all mud dwellers able to survive in temperatures higher than 20°C. Many clams living in these conditions are specially adapted to survive by anaerobic (oxygenless) respiration, living for as long as 8 days without oxygen. The sediment which accumulates around the mangrove roots is a

3

LITTORINES   THE MANGROVE SWAMP

composition of mud and clay, rich in tannin, a natural by-product of the *rhizophora* (mangrove), sulphur and anaerobic bacteria; all devoid of any pathogenic microbes. This is the healthiest of marine environments and reputed for its healing virtues in skin disease. The roots are festooned with a variety of spirographs, sponges, edible oysters, and multiple food sources for molluscs. They are the favoured hatcheries for shells, fish and many other forms of marine life.

Marine meadows

Eel grass invaded the sea from the land, and is found on the seaward side of mangrove swamps and enclosed bays; the roots have actually raised the substratum in many areas. Colonisation has taken place in a depth from the tideline to 5 fathoms. This marine jungle is home to a wide variety of clam and snail species and the grassy blades covered with parasites are abundant food supplies for conchs, seaslugs, cones, sea urchins and pen shells. When *holothuri* (sea cucumbers) live in this habitat it indicates unhealthy algae and an impoverished molluscan fauna, as the animal is a scavenger of dead marine matter.

FLAT TREE OYSTER, *Isognomon alatus*

ANGULATE PERIWINKLE, *Littorina angulifera*

NASSARIUS MUD SNAILS

BEADED PERIWINKLE, *Tectarius muricatus*

The subtidal zone

The Continental Shelf and coral reef represent this zone, where intertidal rocks and cliffs plunge into the sea to clear sand several feet below water level. Here we encounter madrepore and coral. This is the beginning of a complex food chain in tropical waters, responsible for a wide variety of life forms which includes crabs, shrimps and fish where waters are clear and necessarily well oxygenated. Many species of seashells live in this environment and are influenced by the amount of light filtering through the water to them and the proximity of coral blocks beneath which they remain hidden during the day. Molluscan fauna is extremely rich here, and includes tritons, tuns, cowries and spindle shells.

The molluscan phylum

According to their anatomy, marine molluscs are divided into the 7 following groups:

Monoplacophora Neopilina

This is an ancient group of deep water animals, the type *neopilina* is a blind limpet-like univalve measuring 1 inch with a symmetrical, segmented, bilateral body and radula (a rasping, tongue-like organ). It has no eyes or tentacles.

Polyplacophora Chiton or Coat-of-Mail

These molluscs are symmetrical along their length, measuring ¼ to 4 inches. The animal has a creeping foot on its underside. The dorsal shell is composed of 8 calcareous jointed valves, held together by a girdle which may be topped with tufts or hairlike bristles. It has no eyes or tentacles. The sexes are separate and fertilisation is external; the egg masses are jelly-like and disperse quickly. The animal is very slow moving. Deep water species exhibit richer colours. The group is mostly herbivorous feeding occasionally on worms. Their predators are rats, birds, other molluscs and humans.

Aplacophores Worm Molluscs

A little known family of molluscs, whose mantles are covered with scales and spines. There is no shell and the foot which is found on the underside, is grooved. The group is very primitive and the members do not have a distinct head, although they do have a radula. They are either hermaphroditic or of separate sexes and are found from the littoral zone to the abyss. Those interested in this strange family should refer to the Museum of Comparative Zoology, Harvard, MEMOIRS, VOL. 45 pp. 1-260, with 54 plates.

Gastropoda Univalves or Snails

This is the most important group in the phylum, and includes limpets, conchs, whelks, winkles and shell-less seaslugs. The animal is usually spirally coiled and not symmetrical. The lateral development of the embryonic stage is responsible for the twisted shape of the soft body and the shell. The twist of the body is nearly always right-handed, although the *busycon* or turnip snail is known

FUZZY CHITON, *Acanthopleura granulata*

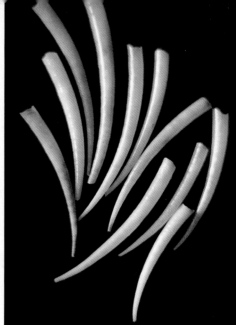

LAMELLOSE WENTLETRAP,
Epitonium lamellosum

MERIDIAN TUSK, *Dentalium meridionale*

to be left-handed, in most other species this is extremely rare. Most gastropods have eyes, tentacles, a nerve system and a well developed anatomy with a muscular creeping foot supporting the operculum or "trap door", and a shell-secreting mantle. The mouth area or buccal cavity has jaws and a radula or "tongue" for feeding. Gills for breathing are within the mantle cavity.

The animals are either deep-sea (benthic) or surface drifting (planktonic) as with sea butterflies, the *pteropods*. Their sizes range from ⅛th of an inch (*bittium* and *vitrinellidae*) to 25 inches (tritons, helmets and conchs). They have a great variety of feeding mechanisms and are either carnivore, herbivore, omnivore (mixed feeding) or parasitic feeders. The sexes are usually separate other than the hermaphroditic *nudibranch* or seaslug family. Gastropods live from above the splash zone to the abyss.

Scaphopoda Tusk Shells

In Latin the word signifies a boat-like foot. The tusk shell is a simple cylindrical tapering tube, pierced at both ends. The animal is symmetrical along its length and the eyeless head and foot have long filaments of miniature hairs for feeding which project from the large

9

Gastropods – Univalves

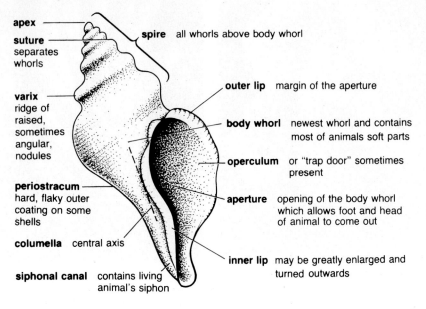

apex

suture separates whorls

spire   all whorls above body whorl

varix ridge of raised, sometimes angular, nodules

outer lip   margin of the aperture

body whorl   newest whorl and contains most of animals soft parts

operculum   or "trap door" sometimes present

periostracum hard, flaky outer coating on some shells

aperture   opening of the body whorl which allows foot and head of animal to come out

columella   central axis

inner lip   may be greatly enlarged and turned outwards

siphonal canal   contains living animal's siphon

front opening. It uses its inflatable foot for burrowing. Caribbean species rarely exceed 2 inches. The sexes are separate and fertilisation is external. They live from the intertidal zone to the abyss.

Pelecypoda or *Lamellibranch*   Bivalves or Clams

Members of this family are the oysters, mussels, scallops, tellins, shipworms, and all two valved shells. These valves may be equal or unequal in size, and are held together by a strong elastic ligament forming a hinge, surmounted by an embryonic apex called an umbo or beak. The beak may have a series of teeth fitting one into the other, which can be used for identification of a species. The animal has a soft flattened body, and a foot which is used for digging and submergence. Many have sensory tentacles and eyes.

Sedentary species often secrete tough threads with which they attach themselves to their chosen base. Being filter feeders, some are able to swim by pumping water through their feeding syphons. The sexes are usually separate, but alternate hermaphrodism exists. The longest living bivalve shell is the Giant Pacific Clam, *Tridacna maxima*, which can live to be over 100 years old.

Pelecypoda – Bivalves

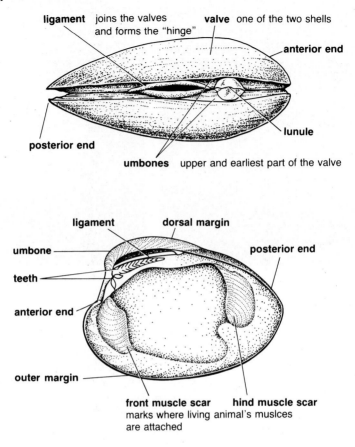

ligament joins the valves and forms the "hinge"

valve one of the two shells

anterior end

posterior end

lunule

umbones upper and earliest part of the valve

ligament

dorsal margin

umbone

posterior end

teeth

anterior end

outer margin

front muscle scar **hind muscle scar**
marks where living animal's muslces
are attached

Cephalopoda Octopus, Squid, Cuttlefish

The most advanced of the molluscan animals, closely approaching the vertebrate realm. They have highly developed heads, brains and eyes and are ferocious, agile and rapid; using jet propulsion. They are mainly pelagic, living in the open sea. With parrot-like beaks, they tear into their preys' flesh, inflicting poisonous bites. They can learn and remember, possessing the largest single nerve fibre in the animal kingdom.

The sexes are separate, and females larger than males. The eggs are often laid in ''sea mops'' containing a few to several hundred eggs.

11

COON OYSTER, *Ostrea frons*   COMMON SPIRULA, *Spirula spirula*

Oceanic squids lay sausage shaped egg masses, containing hundreds of thousand of embryos. Shallow water octopuses of the Caribbean select dens consisting of bottles, cans, dead shells or rocky crevices. The females brood their young there until safely hatched; many mothers die of starvation and exhaustion, sacrificing themselves entirely to the protection of a new generation.

The octopus is the oceans' foremost shell collector, thriving on a continuous diet of molluscs and crustaceans whose empty shells litter its den. Most commonly observed is the *spirula*, whose disused pearly skeleton is blown onto windward beaches of tropical shores all year round; these are minute animals compared with the others in this group. Giant squids live deep in the ocean and can measure up to 50 ft. All cephalopods are capable of immediate colour change, made possible by pigment sacs of innervated chromatophores and other sheen giving cells.

Reproduction and development

Molluscs reproduce in many different ways and are either of separate sexes, or hermaphroditic with the animal starting life as a male to become predominantly female with maturity. They are either oviparous, laying eggs that hatch independently, or viviparous, retaining and incubating the eggs within the female, sometimes in a special incubation pocket, and expelling the young later. With each breeding season an individual female lays millions of eggs either in strands or capsules deposited in masses or singly on solid supports. Some molluscs manage to lay their eggs on their own shells.

The primitive chitons and tusk shells reproduce by simultaneous emission of eggs and sperm into the water by male and female, with immediate fertilisation. In more advanced molluscan families the male has a penis with sperm sac. *Cephalopods* or octopuses transform a chosen tentacle into a male sexual organ which can be severed if necessary during reproduction. Some have fully functioning organs of both sexes and are able to reproduce independently and fertilise their own eggs. Females often have larger shells in order to house swollen sex organs and young when these are born in the mantle cavity. Bivalves have a pair of sex organs, one male and one female. Both organs discharge into the water simultaneously, and often after fertilisation the eggs return to the gill cavity to be released later as free swimming larvae.

According to these different methods of reproduction, the cells of the fertilised eggs start dividing within 3 or 4 hours. The cell division is diagonal rather than parallel to the axis. This primitive trocophore larval stage resembles a cylinder with a girdle of many fine hairs which helps it to swim through the ocean. The trocophore is highly vulnerable and faces a perilous phase of its existence. Sudden changes in water temperature and salinity, or the presence of many predators will spell doom. Fortunately this period in its life is brief, and rarely exceeds more than 4 hours before a first protective shell starts to form.

The most common larval stage in molluscs is that of the veliger, which in many cases bypasses the momentary trocophore stage. This free swimming larva has a tiny prodisoconch (in bivalves) or protoconch (in snails or gastropods) a rudimentary embryonic shell with eyes, tentacles, foot and operculum, or "trap door". The veliger has two strong lobes resembling elephant ears on either side of its head, which are fringed with numerous microscopic hairs (cilia). This

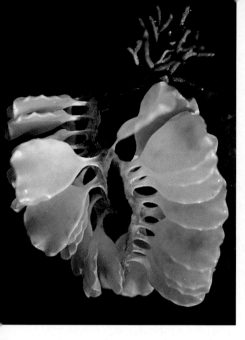

FASCIOLARIA EGG CASES   HORN SHELL SPAWN

line of hairs is called the velum and is an important swimming aid. The veliger spins through the water, carried by tides and currents. Feeding on minute food particles, its pelagic life may last a few days or several weeks. When the growing shell has become too heavy, the veliger sheds its lobes and drops to the bottom of the ocean, where it starts life as an immature member of a crawling or sedentary molluscan world.

At all stages larvae and embryos are the prey of filter feeders, bivalves, corals, crabs, shrimps, and all pelagic animals. Less than one dozen in a thousand will survive attack and assure the following generation. Repopulation records are held by the minute intertidal *hydrobia* snail, a mud dweller whose performance exceeds that of all others in the animal kingdom, by colonising one square foot of the littoral with as many as 10,000 individuals.

Juvenile seashells are not often seen in their environment as they remain hidden under rocks, coral and sand, and occasionally adhere to the mother's operculum, until they are sufficiently developed to fend for themselves. In a few cases they do not resemble the parent. Young conchs resemble cones. They have thin transparent shells with straight lips, and are called "rollers". Young cowrie shells are easily confused with wide mouthed bubble shells. Most molluscs nonetheless produce young that are perfect replicas of themselves.

14

The molluscan body is divided into four regions; cephalic (the head area), visceral (the soft internal organs), mantle (the body's shell-secreting outer layer) and foot. Gastropods have well developed eyes and sensitive feeler tentacles, with the snout or proboscis hiding an intricate ribbon-like serrated tongue called the radula. The serrations on the tongue are a series of efficient teeth used for scraping, rasping, drilling, boring the shells of prey and for feeding in general. Each species has typical radula which is sure proof of identity. Bivalves have no distinct head, this is often replaced for example in oysters and clams, by a series of light sensitive eyes and tentacles which emerge like a fringe around the margin of the open shell. They have a small flat foot and plate-like gills for breathing. The soft body mass contains all the vital organs, which are protected by the mantle or mantle margins.

The protective mantle is also the site for the development of the shell itself. The shape of the soft body of the animal determines the shape of the shell; the even or uneven distribution of the mantle along shell edges, its growth, fragility or solidity. The profuse mantle of the cowrie is able to produce its brilliant shell. The thick fleshy inner mantles of bivalves protect their porcelain and pearl surfaces.

The gastropod foot is used for locomotion, to envelop its prey, to burrow, and occasionally is expanded into wings for swimming. It has a horny or lime operculum, or "trap door", which when the animal withdraws into its shell often seals the aperture. The operculum can also be used as a weapon.

SCHEMATIC OF MOLLUSCAN ANIMAL ATLANTIC UMBRELLA SHELL, *Umbraculum umbraculum, cephalic, visceral, mantle, foot*

FLAME HELMET, *Cassis flammea*

GASTROPOD COLOUR and PIGMENTATION

Colour and pigmentation in shell and animal

Molluscs possess many diverse forms of pigment in both body and shell. Colours and patterns are created according to the animal's diet. The nutrients from the food eaten are broken down as they travel through the blood stream towards the mantle, where they are transformed into highly concentrated cells which are used for the colouration and pigmentation of the structural layers of the shell itself. Each shell is unique and may often bear the same pattern and colour as the animal builder.

The basic shell pigments are melanins and porphyrins, giving colours of indigo, blue, red, orange and yellow. The pigment cells are not altogether stable and are built up intermittently and in concentrations along the mantle edges. The groups of pigment cells produce clusters, dashes, dots, stripes and colours. The high or low number of these cells present in each species, together with molluscan rest periods, will regulate the shell pattern. The colouration of an individual is affected by changing water conditions and increases in salinity or pollution.

16

The organic composition of seashells

Seashells are made up of several layers of crystalline calcium compounds. The innermost layer is calcite, with following cross-lining layers of argonite, which are covered by a final layer of prismatic calcite. All of this is often protected by an outer horny sheath of the protein conchiolin, which is usually called the periostracum. This final, hard, flaky layer often helps with camouflage.

This complex composition is made possible by the chemical content of the animal's blood, which has a high concentration of liquid salt. The mantle is able to concentrate calcium by an osmotic process and immediate crystallisation then takes place between the existing shell layer and mantle cavity. The prismatic structure created in this way resembles laminated sheets and minute bricks which are held together by a mortar made of the protein, conchiolin. The animal carefully repairs damage incurred to any part of its shell.

Seasonal growth is observed by lines and breaks on body whorls; during active growth periods the mollusc dissolves unwanted spines or projections which might hinder feeding or movement. Shells develop rapidly in tropical seas, thickening with age, but remain unchanged once the animal is sexually mature. Abnormally large shells therefore imply a severe parasitic infestation, where the molluscs' sexual organs have been destroyed and so shell growth has not been inhibited.

The great diversity of shapes and colours in seashells would seem to point to a natural selection and an attempt to increase chances of survial.

Cautionary note

Wherever you choose to hunt for shells in the West Indies it is advisable to acquaint yourself first with any local laws and regulations regarding the collection of seashells before you start. Local Immigration, Customs and Post Office personnel will gladly inform you of limits, closed seasons and protected species. When searching for shells, the rocks and corals under which they hide should always be returned to their initial positions as sunlight will rapidly kill all underlying fauna. Juveniles, spawning females and live broken shells should not be removed from the water. Overcollection should be avoided.

The Common Octopus is a willing helper to the shell collector, their dens are often decorated with heaps of attractive species. Be warned, however, as such crevices may also be home to the spotted eel, who when disturbed can bite and hang on tenaciously, such a wound may quickly become infected. It would be sensible to use a stick or probe for such investigations. The scorpion fish although totally unaggressive, remaining immobile and remarkably camouflaged on shallow bottoms, is the bearer of extremely venomous dorsal spines, and should a diver inadvertently receive a puncture wound it is advisable to seek immediate medical attention. Black long spined sea urchins and fire coral should be avoided, provoking unpleasant stings and burns if touched.

All these problems may be minimised by using good gloves and wearing shirts and jeans, or a wet suit. Night diving reveals a beautiful and rare submarine world, as nearly all marine fauna is nocturnal. It is, however, definitely a group activity for the sake of safety.

Finally, few records exist of attacks by sharks, barracudas or sting rays in the Caribbean, when shells are the divers' focus of attention.

Cleaning and preserving seashells

Before using any of the following methods of emptying seashells, try adding a few drops of magnesium chloride to the water in which they are kept; this will eventually relax and drug the animal.

Boiling
Place shell tip-down in shallow cold water, bring to the boil and allow to simmer for 10 to 20 minutes according to size. When both shell and animal have cooled, extract the meat by using a skewer, fork or wire and pulling gently in a clockwise movement. All bivalve shells open within a few minutes when boiled.

Freezing
Place the shell in a freezer compartment for 2 or 3 days. Defrost the shell by holding it under running water or in a bucket of seawater. Extract the soft parts as described above.

Plastic bag
Recommended for travellers. Place the shells in sealed plastic bag, where the humidity and lack of oxygen will rapidly decompose the soft parts; sealing the bag tightly also avoids any smell. Flush the shells out later with a high pressure hose or running water. Rinsing in the sea is equally effective.

Formaldehyde
Available at pharmacies, this may be used at 10% strength for soaking small shells for 24 hours, longer causes blanching. It may also be used on cotton wool to plug a shell and eliminate lingering odours. A further clean plug may be added later. A buffered solution of 70% formalin may be used in laboratory conditions for conserving soft parts needed for analysis or dissection.

Patience is certainly the greatest requirement for cleaning any seashell. Many have coraline deposits and encrustations together with parasitic growth which may be removed with dental tools, probes, and small sharp instruments. Such shells will benefit from soaking in bleach; 1 hour if used undiluted and longer, up to 24 hours, if diluted to 50%. Specimens should be thoroughly rinsed afterwards. The periostracum will dissolve with this treatment, so if you wish to keep it, the shell should only be brushed. Muriatic acid should be used sparingly and applied with a small brush. Rinse thoroughly at once; the chemical not only dissolves foreign matter but the shell itself. Care should be taken not to chip lips and spines during the cleaning process as these represent the value of a specimen. Operculums should be replaced in apertures.

Once prepared the best way to preserve shells is to apply a mixture of mineral oil and ether at 50%. The ether allows the oil to penetrate all shell layers, and will enhance the appearance of the dowdiest specimens. This treatment retains colours and lustre for long periods, and may be repeated.

The proper cataloguing of a shell collection greatly improves its worth. Data written on labels placed with the shell and if possible an accompanying ledger, should include species number, name, locality, depth found, date collected and general observations. Shells will fade with light, and are best protected in collection boxes, cabinets or drawers. Because of this, most museums have only small displays on view to the public.

Many details of molluscan life are still unknown to science. Observations in aquariums are rewarding and photography of the living animal is highly recommended.

 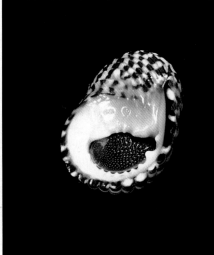

Conchs, helmets, cones and other snails — the univalves

Limpets *Fissurellidae and Acmaeidae*

Limpets are a highly successful family of archaeogastropods, which may be divided into two main groups, Keyhole and True Limpets. They are widely distributed in tropical and temperate seas with most species living attached to the rocks of the splash zone or intertidal areas of our coasts. They are related to many other subfamilies which may live as deep as 800 fathoms. Some are finely and intricately sculptured, but rarely exhibit important colour patterning other than dark rays. Colourful fleshy mantles may enfold species living under coral rubble in shallow or deep water. All have strong radulae (tongues) with which they feed when browsing on algae covered rocks. Their role in coastal erosion is remarkable since their appearance in the Caribbean 25 million years ago. The predators of this family are sea birds, other gastropods and humans.

Genus *Fissurella* Bruguière, 1789

Knobby Keyhole Limpet *Fissurella nodosa*
1 to 2 inches   Lower Florida Keys, West Indies
An abundant species with 20 to 22 strong nodulose ribs. Shell chalky white with glossy white interior. The distinctive keyhole perforation forward of the apex is the exit for the siphoned current of water. Forms colonies on intertidal rocks.

Genus *Acmaea* Eschsholtz, 1830

Spotted Limpet *Acmaea pustulata*
¼ to 1 inch   S.E. Florida, West Indies
This true limpet is cup shaped with a delicate and beautifully patterned shell, liberally spotted with red. The shell can be seen through the transparent, filament edged mantle that cloaks it. The shell is variable in height, its interior is white with a brown callus. They usually adhere to smooth surfaces. The sexes are separate and breeding takes place during the summer months, juveniles reach maturity the following Spring.

(Left) KNOBBY KEYHOLE LIMPET,
Fissurella nodosa

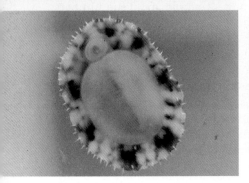

SPOTTED LIMPET, *Acmaea pustulata*

DWARF SUCK-ON LIMPET, *Acmaea leucopleura*

Dwarf Suck-on Limpet   *Acmaea leucopleura*

½ inch   S.E. Forida, West Indies

This species is often found living like a parasite on the shell of a host that will provide its black and white rayed shell perfect camouflage. Here its host is the West Indian Top Shell, *Cittarium pica*. The interior of the shell has a dark brown thickened callus. The animal lives on exposed shores, and as with all other members of the family, feeds at night.

Genus *Diodora* Gray, 1821

Dyson's Keyhole Limpet   *Diodora dysoni*

1 inch   S.E. Florida, West Indies, Brazil

This species is greyish-white with dark rays, the shell is a sculpture of numerous radiating ribs and concentric threads. The foot of the animal invariably reflects the shell pattern and colour. It lives under rocks and rubble from the intertidal zone to a depth of 8 fathoms.

DYSON'S KEYHOLE LIMPET, *Diodora dysoni*

BLEEDING TOOTH, *Nerita peloronta*

Nerites *Neritidae*

Neritidae live in large colonies on the rocky shores of all our islands; some members have migrated inland and up estuaries. They are most abundant where wave action incorporates abundant oxygen into the water. Most are vegetarians feeding nocturnally. They lay egg capsules on semi-exposed rocks.

Genus *Nerita* Linné, 1758

Bleeding Tooth   *Nerita peloronta*

1 to 2 inches   S.E. Florida, West Indies, Brazil

The largest and most beautiful of the Caribbean nerites; the body whorl has variable zigzag markings of red, black, yellow or white and the porcelain of the inner lip has 2 seemingly blood-stained teeth. The operculum has an arm-like projection and the brown coloured soft parts of the animal have similar stains to that of the inner lip.

EMERALD NERITE and COMMON JANTHINA, *Smaragdia viridis and Janthina janthina*

Genus *Smaragdia* Issel, 1869

Emerald Nerite or **Green Lucky**   *Smaragdia viridis*
¼ inch   S.E. Florida, West Indies, Brazil
Both shell, animal and operculum of this tiny nerite are bright green,
an unusual colour for molluscs but which may be caused in this case
by the animal's preference for feeding on the upper section of eel grass
fronds which are the same colour, rather than their base which is
yellowish brown. The smooth, white speckled emerald shell is more
easily spotted in drift sand on beaches than in its environment. The
animal lays delicate circular strings of white egg masses.

Top Shells   *Trochidae*

Genus *Cittarium* Philippi, 1847

West Indian Top Shell, Whelk or **Burgos**   *Cittarium pica*
2 to 5 inches   S.E. Florida, West Indies
The most representative of all Caribbean Top Shells, this species
inhabits the tide pools and rocky shores of exposed coasts. An
important food source for early man, it has become extinct in certain

northern regions and Bermuda. It is mostly algae feeding, although small crabs have been found in the gut. The heavy shell is blue-black with pink and white zigzag markings, a wide pearly aperture and horny circular operculum. The animal clings steadfastly to the surfaces of rocks and crevices with a thick muscular creamy foot. The jet black head has eye stalks that are split into two lobes, the outer one with a single eye.

The empty shell of this species is preferred above all others as an adopted home for the land crab *Coenobita cyleatus*. Because of this West Indian Top Shells may be seen climbing sugar apple trees where the crabs feed on the fruit. The crab inhabitant is itself a favourite bait for fishermen, mounds of its broken shells are found in fishing grounds. As it grows, the crab descends from mountain haunts in search of a larger shell on the sea shore and lives temporarily in shared burrows with others of the family. "Oubliettes" or subterranean dungeons, infamous during the days of slavery, were feared by prisoners largely because of their infestation by these crabs. The land crabs, then known as "Soldier Crabs" were able to inflict painful bites on the prisoners with their strong pincers.

WEST INDIAN TOP SHELL,
Cittarium pica

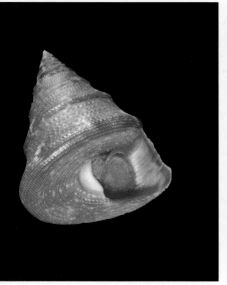
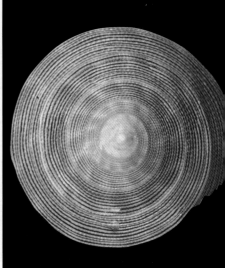

JUJUBE TOP SHELL, *Calliostoma jujubinum*

CHOCOLATE LINED TOP SHELL, *Calliostoma javanicum*

Genus *Calliostoma* Swainson, 1840

Jujube Top Shell   *Calliostoma jujubinum*
1 to 2 inches   Lower Florida Key, West Indies
This species lives on the underside of stones, coral and rubble in calm water. The shell is brownish-red with numerous beaded spiral threads and white markings. The umbilicus is deep and aperture pearly, the animal itself is prune coloured with white speckles.

Chocolate Lined Top Shell   *Calliostoma javanicum*
¾ to 2 inches   Florida to West Indies
An uncommon species occasionally brought from deep water and its usual environment to shallow reefs by hermit crabs. They feed on hard and soft corals, as well as algae. The shell has 6 body whorls with numerous cream and chocolate coloured threads, the animal itself has an identical pattern

26

CHESTNUT TURBAN, *Turbo castanea*

Genus *Turbo* Linné, 1758

Chestnut Turban   *Turbo castaneus*

¾ to 1½ inches   S.E. U.S., West Indies

This species colonises calm, shallow eel grass beds, where it feeds on algae. The shell is chestnut with creamy markings, the globe-shaped body whorl has numerous small, rounded, spiny riblets giving a noduled appearance. The operculum is thick and porcellaneous and either pink or green. The animal is a favoured prey of *Octopus vulgaris.* It is difficult to observe on the sea bed as its thick, mossy periostracum attracts mud and sand particles.

Turbans and Star Shells   *Turbinidae*

These are strong, globe-shaped, solid shells, with smooth or rugged exterior. All members have hard, calcium-rich operculums. As vegetarians, they prefer algae and gather to graze on exposed coastal reefs. The sexes are separate and the eggs are shed directly into the sea. For many centuries top shells have been harvested for the manufacture of mother-of-pearl buttons and other jewellery.

GREEN STAR SHELL, *Astraea tuber*   CARVED STAR SHELL, *Astraea caelata*

Genus *Astraea* Röding, 1798

Green Star Shell   *Astraea tuber*
1 to 2½ inches   Florida Keys, West Indies, Brazil
An abundant species living on or beneath intertidal rocks. The shell
colouring is bright green with bars of red and white on coarse ridge-
like sculpturing. The base is smooth and white, the operculum has
a distinctive comma-like punctuation.

Carved Star Shell   *Astraea caelata*
2 to 3 inches   S.E. Florida, West Indies, Venezuela
A handsome heavy shell with numerous pink and white furrowed
spines on the lower whorls and base. Often heavily encrusted with
parasitic growth. Thick, white, pimpled limy operculum. Co-habits
with *Astraea tuber* in similar conditions.

Long Spined Star Shell   *Astraea phoebia*
2 to 4 inches   S.E. Florida, West Indies, Venezuela
Unlike other star shells, *Astraea phoebia* inhabits shallow eel grass
beds. It is a low spired shell with a spiral of long triangular spines

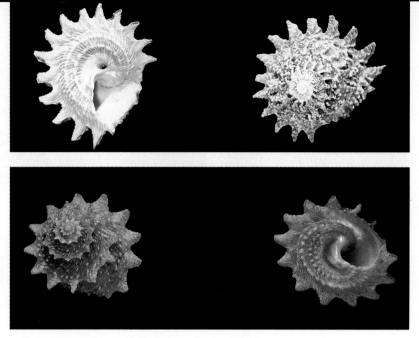

(Top) LONG SPINED STAR SHELL, *Astraea phoebia*
(Above) SHORT SPINED STAR SHELL, *Astraea brevispina*

and green and orange body whorls. Most often well camouflaged with mud and sand particles.

Short Spined Star Shell   *Astraea brevispina*
1½ to 3 inches   West Indies, Venezuela
This species is most frequently encountered in the Southern Caribbean. The handsome shell has numerous golden triangular spines and a high spire, distinguishing it from *A. phoebia.* The base has a rich orange stain at the umbilicus and a red operculum. It often colonises eel grass beds and shallow mud bottoms.

Littorines or Periwinkles   *Littorinidae*
Littorines or Periwinkles are a highly successful family of snails from which the world's littoral or shore-line, draws its name. They are not brightly coloured, but tend to blend into their environment. They are vegetarians, each with its preferred algal diet. Although strictly marine animals, some are able to live out of water, exposed to extreme heat for many weeks at a time, breathing atmospheric air. They are a favourite prey of shore birds. Reproductive methods are varied and the eggs are either shed freely or in floating capsules of jellylike masses, or retained in the female until ready to hatch.

29

ANGULATE PERIWINKLE, *Littorina angulifera*

BEADED PERIWINKLE, *Tectarius muricatus*

Genus *Littorina* Férussac, 1822

Angulate or **Mangrove Periwinkle** *Littorina angulifera*
1 to 1½ inches   S. Florida and West Indies
A thin, translucent but solid shell with a sculpturing of numerous
fine spiral lines. The body colour is buff, yellow or red, and the
operculum thin and horny. The females are larger than males with
long delicate tentacles used to detect obstacles. They move rapidly,
leaving behind them a trail of mucus. The species is a native of the
flooded tropical mangrove forest, living on dry branches and roots.
They are also found on wood pilings.

Genus *Tectarius* Valenciennes, 1833

Beaded Periwinkle *Tectarius muricatus*
½ to 1 inch   Lower Florida Keys, West Indies
A pale grey blue shell with strongly beaded sculpturing. It lives high
above the tide line, where it resists maximum exposure to heat and
desiccation, remaining stationary for many weeks. It has been
observed to live on Prickly Pear cacti, *Opuntia dillenii*, but is not
thought to feed on them. Nonetheless the thorny cacti provide the

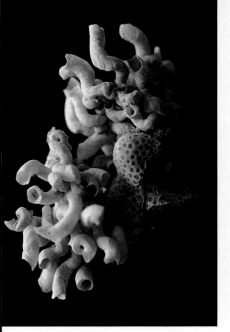

WORM SHELL, *Petaloconchus*

KNORR'S WORM SHELL,
Vermicularia knorri

perfect protection from predators. The periwinkle returns to the splash zone to breed. Many of today's land snails evolved from sea-living ancestors, transforming their breathing apparatus accordingly. The life-style of the periwinkle suggests how this evolution might have taken place.

Worm Shells and Turitellas   *Turitellidae*

Genus *Vermicularia* Lamarck, 1799

Worm Shells   *Petaloconchus*
Worm shells portray a definite departure from the normal gastropod spiral shape. Beginning life in an orthodox manner as members of the Superfamily *Certhiacea*, they subsequently end up in free flowing forms and inextricable, tangled masses, attached to rock and coral bases. Possessing operculums they are filter feeders and face the ocean where there is constant water change and renewal of oxygen. The species illustrated is from the Southern Caribbean. It is attached to the star coral *Monastrea cavernosa*.

31

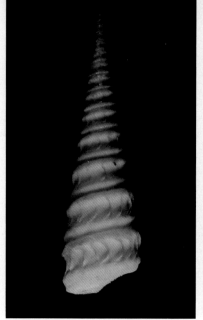

EASTERN TURRET SHELL, *Turitella exoleta*

VARIEGATED TURRET SHELL, *Turitella variegata*

Genus *Turitella* Lamarck 1799

Eastern Turret Shell   *Turitella exoleta*
2 to 4 inches   S. Carolina and Caribbean
A long tapering shell whose numerous buff or white body whorls are
decorated with scalelike layers which are divided by deep ridges.
Although of the same family as the bizarrely shaped *petaloconchus*,
the shell shape of the *turitella* is strict and successful. The animal
has a multispiral circular operculum with a central point. It lives as
a burrower in mud and sand from depths of 1 to 100 fathoms.

Variegated Turret Shell   *Turitella variegata*
3 to 5 inches   S.E. Florida, West Indies, Brazil
This species has a tapering shell with deep whorls and spiral threads.
The colour varies from purple-brown to creamy white. A common,
often abundant member of the South American marine fauna found
at depths from 1 to 20 fathoms on mud bottoms from where they
are frequently beached in their thousands by dredging nets. In the
Caribbean they favour estuarine conditions.

QUEEN CONCH, *Strombus gigas*

Conchs *Strombidae*

Strombus are widely distributed throughout the world's tropical regions. Seven species inhabit the marine algae beds of the Caribbean. The Pink Conch *Strombus gigas* is of great economic value, conch meat is nutritious and is a main staple of the diet in the Bahamas. Populations have now been seriously depleted in many areas; in Bermudan waters the capture of any live specimen is illegal. In most islands it is against the law to collect juveniles, and a closed season is in force during the summer months to allow the regrouping animals to reproduce.

All members of this genus have a distinctive "stromboid notch" on the lower part of the outer lip, through which the animal slides its enlarged eye stalk or pedicel. The iris of the eye is composed of numerous coloured concentric circles, and each eye has an accompanying tentacle. The strong muscular foot with its sickle-shaped operculum allows the conch to crawl and hop. Strictly vegetarian, these animals are usually seen grazing on weed in shallow water, but may migrate to depths of 20 fathoms where they live on mud and sand; most of these deep water specimens are mature adults.

The sexes are separate, the male with a long narrow penis behind the right tentacle. The female lays long strings of gelatinous eggs,

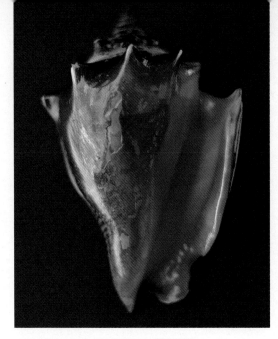

WEST INDIAN FIGHTING CONCH,
Stombus pugilis

which are camouflaged by sand particles which stick to them. A single mass of eggs may contain 700,000 embryos which hatch into free-swimming larvae 3 or 4 days later. The handsome flared lip of the *Strombus gigas* takes 5 years to form.

Living for as long as 25 years the elderly, non-reproductive animal has a shell with its aperture and lip covered by an aluminium sheen. A 2 inch long fish, *Astrapogon stellatus*, lives within the mantle of many Pink Conchs, as a commensal species. As many as 5 of these fishes may live in this retreat at one time, and will expire quickly if removed from their adopted habitat.

Conch shells were used by Amerindians as a durable material for the manufacture of tools, weapons and jewellery. The conch's predators other than man are rays, sharks and pufferfish.

Queen or **Pink Conch**   *Strombus gigas*

8 to 10 inches   South Florida to Brazil

The largest of Caribbean conch shells with pink flaring lip and body whorls. It is vegetarian and lives on eel grass. Juveniles or "rollers" resemble cones and are brightly coloured, often brown with a white zigzag pattern. The juvenile conch is considered immature until its spectacular pink lip has developed.

ROOSTER TAIL CONCH, *Stombus gallus*

West Indian Fighting Conch   *Strombus pugilis*
3 to 4 inches   S.E. Florida to Brazil
The shell of this conch is coloured a rich red-orange to salmon pink
with a velvety periostracum and spines on the body whorls. The outer
lip is expanded but not winged as with other members of this genus.
It colonises eel grass beds from depths of 1 fathom to 20, in channels
on mud bottoms. The animal has a horny saw-edged operculum. It
migrates in the summer and at such times is unfortunately and
inadvertently captured by thousands in fishing nets.

Rooster Tail Conch   *Strombus gallus*
4 to 8 inches   S.E. Florida and West Indies
The least common of Caribbean *strombidae*, it may be found
occasionally either on eel grass beds or in deeper water on sand and
coral from depths of 1 to 8 fathoms. The shell has a distinctive flared
lip with a long channelled extension of the posterior end in adults.
The shell colour is pink, red, yellow, mauve or tan. The operculum
is sickle shaped.

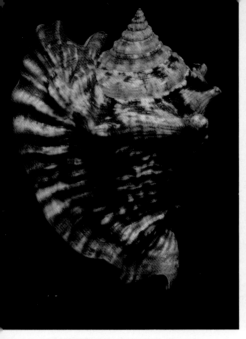 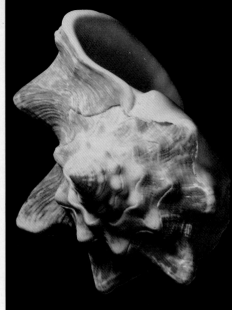

HAWK WING CONCH, *Stombus raninus*

MILK CONCH, *Strombus costatus*

Hawk Wing Conch *Strombus raninus*

2 to 3 inches   S.E. Florida, West Indies

Not to be mistaken for the juvenile of *S. gigas*. The pink edged lip and inner walls of the shell which form a shield, are glazed and may be tinged with green. The body whorls are usually mottled brown or purple. The animal lives in shallow eel grass.

Milk Conch *Strombus costatus*

4 to 9 inches   S.E. Florida, West Indies, Venezuela

A solid, thick lipped shell, with glossy white or cream lip and aperture. The juvenile "roller" stage shells are brilliantly coloured orange, yellow, pink, mauve and red, their lips are thin and transparent. A strawlike periostracum protects the low blunt spines. The animal may have a green stained proboscis (snout) and horny sickle-shaped operculum.

ATLANTIC CARRIER SHELL,
Xenophora conchyliophora
with PENNSYLVANIA
LUCINE, *Lucina pensylvanica*

Carrier Shells *Xenophoridae*

Genus *xenophora* G. Fischer, 1807

Atlantic Carrier Shell *Xenophora conchyliophora*
2 to 3 inches   S. Florida, West Indies to Brazil
An unusual and interesting species. The animal diligently collects
large amounts of marine debris such as sponges, corals, stones and
glass, other molluscs, pottery; in fact any small item that will provide
it with camouflage so that it can resemble a small mound of rubble
or dead shells and so avoid interest from would-be predators. When
it has chosen a new addition to its camouflage it rapidly cements the
new piece to the aperture with a strong gluey secretion, subsequently
remaining motionless for several hours to be sure that the new
addition is properly fixed.

The shell without these appendages is conical with 7 or 8 whorls,
the base has a fine but uneven network of ridges coloured brownish
red on cream. The animal has a scarlet muscular foot which can lift
it 3 inches from the ground when moving forward, making it look
like a clumsy, overloaded mushroom. The animal is nocturnal, living
on shallow sand banks in coral and rubble near reef systems, and on
deeper coral to a depth of 10 fathoms.

FOUR SPOTTED TRIVIA, *Trivia quadripunctata*

Genus *Trivia* Broderip, 1837

Trivia resemble miniature cowries and are small, oval, globe-like shells resembling beans. There are numerous ribs across the shell, and the apertures are narrow and very finely toothed. The animals have fleshy mantles decorated with small papillae which completely cover the shell when the twin lobes meet at the ridge which extends from the front to the back of the shell, across the shell's summit.

Often called Coffee Grains or Good Luck Shells, these shells are common throughout the tropics in shallow and intertidal waters where they live under rocks and rubble. They vary in colour from purest white to dark pink, some bear darker coloured spots. They feed on ascidians (sea squirts) in which they also lay their eggs.

Four Spotted Trivia *Trivia quadripunctata*

½ inch   S.E. Florida, West Indies

Bright pink with 4 brown spots on the back of the shell. The shell is sculptured with 20 to 24 riblets. The animal has a beautiful mantle which is deep purple with tiny, greyish white papillae. It lives under intertidal rubble.

MEASLE COWRIE, *Cypraea zebra*

MEASLE COWRIE, *Cypraea zebra*, living animal

Cowries   *Cypraeidae*

The lustrous cowrie shell with its slender toothed aperture has played a magical role in the lives of men for many centuries. Living only in tropical waters they usually establish themselves in ancient, well formed coral reefs, where they remain hidden in deep crevices during the day. They are nocturnal and have diverse feeding habits. The sexes are separate. The juveniles resemble wide mouthed bubble shells. The animal itself far surpasses the beauty of the shell it secretes; the mantle is covered with colourful fringes and tiny papillae which envelop the entire shell. The mantle is responsible for the continued gloss of the shell, and the creation of colour patterns and multicoloured motifs. One of the world's rarest cowries *Cypraea surinamensis* lives in the deep offshore waters of the Caribbean.

Genus *Cypraea* Linné, 1758

Measle Cowrie   *Cypraea zebra*

2 to 4 inches   S.E. Forida, West Indies to Venezuela

This species lives in moderately shallow water in deep crevices to a depth of 15 fathoms. The shells are glossy brown with numerous white spots and circles at the base. The juveniles do not have the

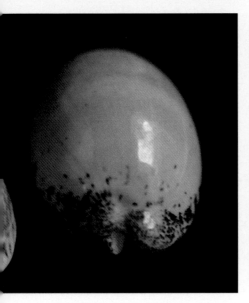 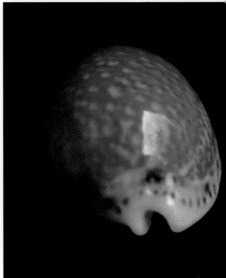

ATLANTIC GREY COWRIE, *Cypraea cinerea*

ATLANTIC YELLOW COWRIE, *Cypraea spurca acicularis*

raised tooth markings on the aperture, and are uni-coloured with pale banding. The animal is one of the most beautiful members of the marine fauna.

Atlantic Grey Cowrie *Cypraea cinerea*
1 to 1½ inches   Florida, West Indies to Venezuela
The shell is brown with darker speckling and a cream coloured base. The animal has a transparent mantle. The females breed in summer and sit protectively on their spawn. The colour of this cowrie fades quickly in beach specimens to light grey.

Atlantic Yellow Cowrie *Cypraea spurca acicularis*
½ to 1 inch   S. Carolina, West Indies to Brazil
Shell bright orange flushed with white, and orange brown spots at the base. The animal has a handsome, frilled mantle. It lives in shallow submerged reef areas to a depth of 12 fathoms and has also been seen living on eel grass beds.

40

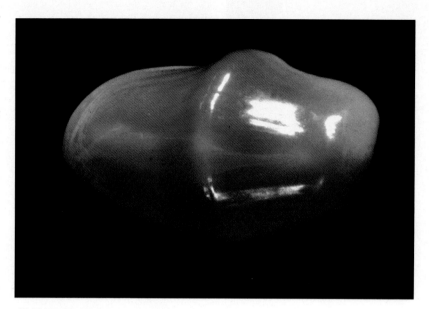

FLAMINGO TONGUE, *Cyphoma gibbosum*

Cyphoma *Ovulidae*

Genus *Cyphoma* Röding, 1798

Flamingo Tongue *Cyphoma gibbosum*
1 to 1¾ inches   S.E. U.S., West Indies, Venezuela
A glossy, tubular, pink shell with a distinctive swollen ridge across the back of the shell. The aperture is long, narrow and smooth. The handsome animal has a rosy mantle which extends onto the shell, displaying numerous black rings which make it easily visible against the soft coral, sea whips and sea fans it lives and feeds on.

This was once a very common species, forming large colonies which were one of the most beautiful sights to be seen on a coral reef. Serious de-population has taken place by over collecting in nearly every part of the Caribbean, and collectors are now asked to observe rather than collect those specimens they do encounter.

Moon Snails *Nacticidae*

These are active sand burrowing nocturnal carnivores, devouring large quantities of other invertebrates daily. They enfold their prey in their large mantles and with an acid secretion and rasping radula teeth, make perfect circular cuts into the shells of their captives in order

41

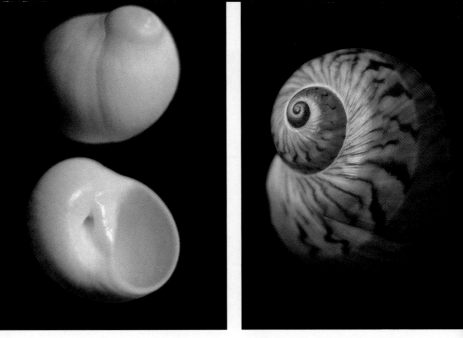

MILK MOON SHELL, *Polinices lacteus*   COLOURFUL ATLANTIC NATICA, *Natica canrena*

to extract the soft meat. The sexes are separate with the female laying sandy egg filled "collars" which have either frilly or straight edges according to the aperture of the species. They make deep furrows as they plough through sand.

Genus *Polinices* Montfort, 1810

Milk Moon Shell   *Polinices lacteus*

½ to 2 inches   West Indies

A globe-shaped, glossy white shell with a wide, deep hollow at the base of the shell. It is distinguished by a wine coloured or amber operculum. It lives submerged in enclosed bays and lagoons, close to coral reefs to a depth of 8 fathoms.

Genus *Natica* Scopoli, 1777

Colourful Atlantic Natica   *Natica canrena*

1 to 3 inches   West Indies to Brazil

A glossy brown shell with numerous wavy zigzag reddish-brown lines on white spiral bands. The base has a wide, deep umbilicus. The animal has a large pink fleshy mantle reflecting its shell pattern. It lives to a depth of 10 fathoms on sand and coral.

COMMON BABY'S EAR, *Sinum perspectivum*

Genus *Sinum* Röding, 1798

Common Baby's Ear   *Sinum perspectivum* Say 1831

1 to 2 inches   West Indies to Brazil

This species is, as the name suggests, shaped like an ear with a wide aperture. The white shell has numerous wavy spiral lines and a straw coloured periostracum. The animal has a minute operculum and such a thick fleshy mantle that it cannot retreat inside its own shell. It lives to depths of 12 fathoms on and in mud and sand.

Helmets, Tritons, Tuns and Frog Shells   *Tonnacea*

The Helmet shells, or *Cassis* family are highly developed members of this group, and extremely active carnivores. They live in coral sediment from the shore line to a depth of 20 fathoms where they prey on star fish and sea urchins. The Helmet shells have a remarkable toothed lip, turned back into a shield, and a strong muscular foot with which they burrow and disappear within seconds. So handsome are the shells of these animals, used for cameo cutting and jewellery, that population numbers have suffered in all tropical waters from over collection. In the South Pacific, Helmet shells have been granted total protection. Their rarity is now apparent in the West Indies and it is hoped that similar laws will be made to allow these animals to

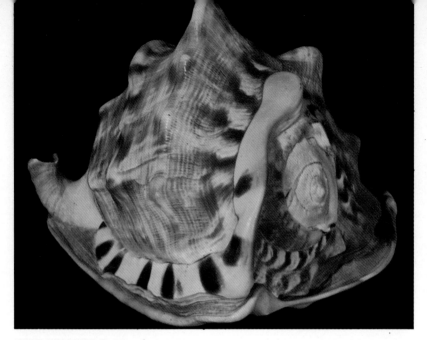

KING HELMET, *Cassis tuberosa*

survive. Helmets are either male or female and thousands of eggs are laid in towerlike constructions.

The smaller Tritons usually have a thick, hairy periostracum concealing lines of well developed knobbly projections; their apertures are toothed and the animals have leopard patterned mantles. They are highly carnivorous and amongst the most aggressive of all molluscs.

Tuns are very different with fragile, globe-like smooth shells. They have no operculums, and some have large midnight blue mantles with which they are able to cover most of the shell.

The *Bursidae* or Frog Shells are sharply angled rock dwellers, with snouts that can lengthen to impressive dimensions when swallowing prey. They are often found heavily encrusted with marine growth which makes the shells difficult to clean.

The legendary Trumpet Triton is found throughout the tropics, and is a formidable predator of starfish and sea urchins. It is protected in the Pacific for two reasons; its usefulness as a scavenger of the fauna which destroys the coral reef, and its entry into the realm of nearly extinct species through over collection. In the Caribbean this beautiful species was once common; its survival now depends on conservation laws made in its favour.

EMPEROR HELMET, *Cassis madagascariensis*

FLAME HELMET, *Cassis flammea*

Genus *Cassis* Scopoli, 1777 — The Helmets

King Helmet *Cassis tuberosa*
7 to 12 inches   S.E. Florida, West Indies to Venezuela
This handsome species and the Queen Conch *S. gigas* are true symbols of the Caribbean. The shell has a highly polished coffee coloured triangular body shield and outer lip, both with strong dark brown teeth, in live specimens there is often an additional purple sheen. The body whorl is cream coloured with numerous brown zigzag markings and three rows of blunt spines. It lives in shallow eel grass and coral to a depth of 8 fathoms.

Emperor Helmet or **Queen Helmet** *Cassis madagascariensis*
4 to 12 inches   West Indies to Brazil
An extremely beautiful species with brilliant flame coloured body shield and outer lip, both with prominent white teeth bordered with dark brown. The body whorl is glossy and cream coloured with numerous longitudinal growth lines and three rows of low spines. The animal lives in deep water on clear sand and coral sediment from depths of 4 to 10 fathoms; single specimens are occasionally seen wandering over shallow eel grass beds.

TRUMPET TRITON, *Charonia variegata*

TRUMPET TRITON, *Charonia variegata*, Living animal

Flame Helmet or **Princess Helmet**   *Cassis flammea*
4 to 8 inches   Florida to Brazil
Smallest of the *cassis* with glossy cream coloured body shield, with white teeth on both outer lip and shield. In South American specimens the shield may be tinged with pink. The tan coloured body whorl has fine growth lines which often appear in a net-like pattern. Living in shallows on eel grass and close to coral reef systems, this helmet may reach the size of an adult *C. tuberosa* (the King helmet) in certain areas.

Genus *Cymatium* Röding, 1798 — The Tritons

Trumpet Triton or **Corn of Abundance**   *Charonia variegata*
10 to 18 inches   S.E. Florida, West Indies, Venezuela
This magnificent shell is usually brown with numerous zigzag markings of mauve, black or darker colours on the spiral whorls, rare bright orange-red specimens are valuable. Tritons have been observed living from the shore under rocky outcrops to depths of 20 fathoms on soft sand and mud. These deep water specimens are always mature adults.

46

ATLANTIC HAIRY TRITON,
Cymatium pileare martinianum

GOLD MOUTHED TRITON,
Cymatium nicobaricum

If the end of a shell (the spire) is cut off, it may be blown like a trumpet or horn.

Atlantic Hairy Triton   *Cymatium pileare martinianum*
2 to 5 inches   Florida, West Indies to Venezuela
The shell is orange or dark brown with white banded spiral sculpturing. The aperture has a double row of paired teeth. The animal is leopard patterned with a horny oval operculum. It lives under rocks from the shoreline to a depth of 8 fathoms. Its prey are crabs and other invertebrates.

Gold Mouthed Triton   *Cymatium nicobaricum*
1 to 4 inches   S. E. Florida, West Indies
Grey or occasionally orange shell with darker mottling of body whorls. Orange aperture. Distinguished from *C. pileare* by the single row of paired teeth decorating the aperture of this shell. It lives under shallow rocks and colonises the soft mud of mangrove swamps.

 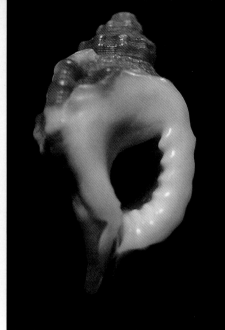

DOG HEAD TRITON, *Cymatium caribbaeum*

KNOBBY TRITON, *Cymatium muricinum*

Dog Head Triton   *Cymatium caribbaeum*

1½ to 3 inches   S. E. Florida, West Indies, Venezuela
A more bulbous shell than the others of the genus, with a long
siphonal canal. The body whorl is decorated with strong spiral cords
and white varices. The outer lip has 7 or 8 thick white teeth. The
animal has a spotted mantle, an oval operculum and a long ridged
hairy periostracum. It lives under coral heads in sand near coral reef
systems from a depth of 1 to 12 fathoms.

Knobby Triton   *Cymatium muricinum*

1 to 2 inches   Florida, West Indies to Brazil
The shell is dull rough white, mottled or uniformly brown, often with
a central band. The body whorls are knobbed and the body shield
glossy white with an orange or wine coloured interior. The siphonal
canal is extended and curves backwards. The animal lives on mud
and sand and in estuaries at depths from 1 to 8 fathoms.

48

ANGULAR TRITON, *Cymatium femorale*

GRANULAR FROG SHELL, *Bursa granularis*

Angular Triton *Cymatium femorale*
3 to 6 inches   Florida, West Indies to Venezuela

A beautiful triangular shaped shell with heavy brown axial ribbing across the shell and white knobby markings. The aperture is often mauve in juveniles, otherwise white. The animal itself is lavender coloured with brown speckles and a minute operculum. The periostracum is thick and matted. The animal favours a shallow eel grass environment and occasionally coral sand. It is found at depths from 1 to 15 fathoms.

Genus *Bursa* Röding 1798 — The Frog Shells

Granular Frog Shell *Bursa granularis*
2 to 2¾ inches   Florida, West Indies to Brazil

The shell is brown with numerous beads on the body whorls. The pleated body shield is orange or cream; the shell's outer lip is thick and toothed. The animal lives submerged under rocks and in crevices to depths of 15 fathoms.

ST. THOMAS FROG SHELL, *Bursa thomae*

SCOTCH BONNET, *Phalium grdnulatum*

St. Thomas Frog Shell *Bursa thomae*

1 to 2½ inches   West Indies to Brazil

This species is easily distinguished from the others in the genus by its bright mauve aperture. Its body whorls are knobbed but usually covered and disguised by heavy encrustations. It lives under coral heads and in crevices at depths from 2 to 15 fathoms.

Genus *Phalium* Link 1807 — The Bonnets

Scotch Bonnet *Phalium granulatum*

2 to 4 inches   N. Carolina, West Indies to Venezuela

The body whorls of this shell may be smooth or spirally grooved. The colour is cream with several rows of brown squares. The aperture is glossy white and pimpled, the outer lip is toothed. The operculum is thin and fan shaped. It is a sand loving species found under coral heads from depths of 1 to 8 fathoms.

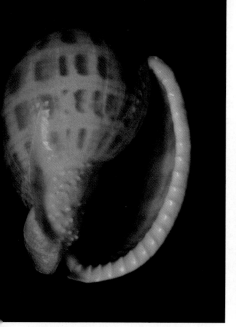

SMOOTH SCOTCH BONNET,
Phalium cicatricosum

RETICULATED COWRIE SHELL,
Cypraecassis testiculis

Smooth Scotch Bonnet *Phalium cicatricosum*

2 to 4 inches   Florida, West Indies to Brazil

Similar to *P. granulatum* but with a smooth, thin and shiny body whorl. The animal has a mantle with a purple sheen and ejects a mauve liquid as a screen to either bluff or deter predators. Found on sand and coral bottoms from depths of 1 to 10 fathoms.

Genus *Cypraecassis* Stutchbury 1837

Reticulated Cowrie Shell or
Reticulated Cowrie Helmet *Cypraecassis testiculus*

1½ to 4 inches   N. Carolina to Brazil

An orange or flame coloured shell with brown banding. The body whorl has numerous parallel folds and ridges, and a network of sculpturing. The aperture is glossy yellow or orange, the outer lip has strong teeth. It lives in subtidal calm waters close to reef systems buried in sand.

Genus *Tonna* Brünnich 1772 — The Tuns

Atlantic Partridge Tun   *Tonna maculosa*
3 to 7 inches   S.E. Florida, West Indies to Venezuela
Shell inflated with numerous spiral cords, and bands of light or dark brown. The outer lip is wavy and notched. The handsome midnight blue animal has a mantle that covers the shell; it does not have an operculum. It lives submerged to a depth of 8 fathoms under coral heads. Deepwater specimens living in mud sediment are often uniformly dark brown.

Murex   *Muricidae*

This is a distinctive family of voracious rock dwellers. Nearly all have strong spines or intricate leaf-like folds, with delicate and elaborate sculpturing, giving them a dimension not found in any other molluscan family. These highly carnivorous animals use their rasping radula teeth and drilling organs with extreme efficiency, patiently piercing the shells and operculums of their prey, taking as long as 5 days to do so if necessary. They will also smother their captives with their strong muscular foot, or use it to apply suction whilst prying open bivalves with the edge of their lips. Many are unselective scavengers feeding on carrion.

A further surprising method of dealing with unyielding prey is often employed particularly on clams. The Murex grips its quarry tightly with its foot and outer lip and then pounds its victim on a hard surface until it has chipped the shell sufficiently to insert its snout and eat the soft parts. Murex will also act jointly to achieve their ends and launch devastating 'raids' on clam beds.

Sexes are separate and females are known to have more than one partner, capable of storing sperm for as long as 14 months; the resulting fertilised embryos may be of mixed parentage. Often egg masses are communal, the young usually leaving the capsules as miniature snails. However, when several eggs are present in a single capsule, the young sometimes display their potential for cannibalism.

Muricidae also include the rock dwelling intertidal *Purpura patula* and *Thais deltoidea*. *Purpura patula* has a unique glandular secretion which is strong smelling and greenish yellow. It is very likely that this is used by the snail as a drug to paralyse chitons and limpets, so allowing their removal from rocks, an otherwise impossible task. The liquid rapidly turns purple and becomes the substance purpurin, the chemical pigment used for the Royal Tyrian Purple dye, and closely related to natural indigo. In the New World, Mayas and Aztecs milked this mollusc repeatedly to extract the precious dye without

ATLANTIC PARTRIDGE TUN, *Tonna maculosa*, front

ATLANTIC PARTRIDGE TUN, *Tonna maculosa*, dorsal

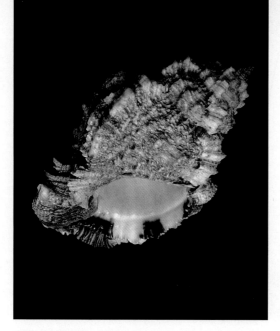

APPLE MUREX, *Murex pomum*

removing the shell from its environment. On the Pacific coast of Mexico fishermen continue this craft of dyeing, carrying skeins of cotton with them for immediate immersion in the liquid. From these skeins the women weave beautiful skirts called "caracollilo"

Apple Murex   *Murex pomum*
2 to 5 inches   Florida to Brazil
A notorious West Indian marine scavenger. The body whorls are tan coloured with rough sculpturing and short spines. The aperture is cream and glossy with a distinctive dark spot. According to age the outer lip may be wavy or toothed. The animal has a thick oval operculum which tightly fits the aperture. It lives in shallow water close to rocks and eel grass and on mud bottoms, to depths of 10 fathoms; deep water specimens are often bright orange-red and outsize.

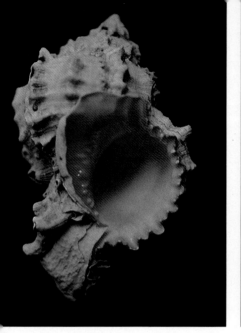
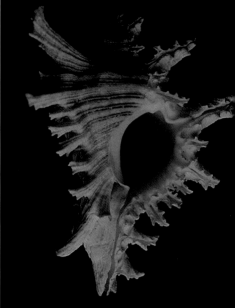

MARGARITA MUREX, *Murex margaritensis*

WEST INDIAN MUREX, *Murex brevifrons*

Margarita Murex   *Murex margaritensis*
2 to 5 inches   Southern Caribbean
An obese murex with a beautiful bright pink or yellow glazed aperture, often with a black stain. The body whorls are chalky white with rough blunt spines on the raised edges. It colonises certain islands off Northern Venezuela to depths of 6 fathoms. It has been observed to breed communally.

West Indian Murex   *Murex brevifrons*
2 to 5 inches   Florida, West Indies to Brazil
This shell is variable in colour from albino to brown-black. The body whorl has spiral ridges and three well developed varices down the length of the shell bearing long spines. The aperture is gaping. This marine snail lives on eel grass and under rocks on mud bottoms down to 6 fathoms.

BENT-BEAK MUREX, *Murex recurvirostris*

WIDE MOUTHED PURPURA, *Purpura patula*

Bent-beak Murex *Murex recurvirostris*

2 to 3 inches   Florida, West Indies to Brazil

A variable species according to environment. Grey, beige or pink body whorls with many small ridges across the shell and blunt spines on the varices. The shell has a distinctive long siphonal canal. The aperture is toothed and circular. It is locally common in the Southern Caribbean on the muddy bottoms of lagoons at depths from 1 to 15 fathoms.

Genus *Purpura* Bruguière 1789

Wide Mouthed Purpura *Purpura patula*

2 to 3½ inches   S.E. Florida, West Indies

The shell has a gaping glossy orange aperture and dark brown stains on the outer lip. The body whorl is grey with rows of sharp nodules, eroding with age. This intertidal species, known for its dye giving properties, is highly carnivorous. Taking prey and feeding is often a group activity and their targets are nerites, limpets and chitons.

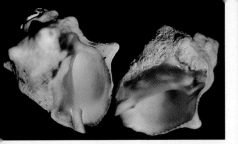

DELTOID ROCK SHELL, *Thais deltoidea*

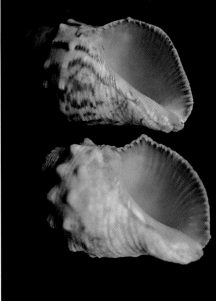

RUSTIC ROCK SHELL, *Thais rustica*

FLORIDA ROCK SHELL, *Thais haemastoma floridana*

Genus *Thais* Röding 1798

Deltoid Rock Shell *Thais deltoidea*

1 to 2 inches   Florida and West Indies

A triangular white shell with black bands of colour and blunt spines on the body whorls, usually covered by parasitic growth. The aperture is white with a bright purple inner lip. It lives intertidally on rocks where it preys on mussels.

Florida Rock Shell *Thais haemastoma floridana*

2 to 4 inches   S.E. U.S. to Venezuela

A highly variable species. The body whorls are finely sculptured with spiral lines and may be coloured grey, or coffee coloured with flecks. The whorls are sometimes noduled. The aperture and lip are cream coloured, but may be orange or scarlet in Trinidad and Venezuela.

Rustic Rock Shell *Thais rustica*

1 to 1½ inches   S.E. Florida and West Indies

Very similar to the above species but smaller with a uniformly cream body shield and outer lip, the interior of which often has a secondary series of ridges within the aperture.

FRILLY DWARF TRITON, *Favartia alveata*

SHORT CORAL SHELL, *Coralliophila abbreviata*

Genus *Favartia* Jousseaume 1880

Frilly Dwarf Triton *Favartia alveata*

½ to 1 inch   Florida, West Indies to Brazil

A small, pretty murex species with 6 or 7 frilled ridges running the length of the shell, and numerous ridges across the shell. The aperture is small and circular with a golden horny operculum. It lives under the rocks of the intertidal zone.

Coral Shells *Magilidae*

Coral Shells are a uniquely parasitic species, living nestled in groups at the base of hard and soft corals where their shells become deformed with coralline growth.

Genus *Coralliophila* H. and A. Adams

Short Coral Shell *Coralliophila abbreviata*

½ to 2 inches   Florida, West Indies to Brazil

A robust rough off white shell with numerous axial ridges. The aperture is stained orange, the operculum tan. It lives on fire and elkhorn coral, where it lives in parasitic colonies. The eggs are bright orange and laid in disorderly masses.

CARIBBEAN CORAL SHELL,
Coralliophila caribaea

COMMON DOVE SHELL, *Columbella mercatoria*

Caribbean Coral Shell *Coralliophila caribaea*
½ to 1 inch   S. Carolina, Florida, West Indies to Brazil
More triangular than the former with a lavender coloured aperture,
and fewer ridges across the shell. It lives in colonies on gorgonia, other
soft corals and madrepore. Neither Coral Shells have radulas and
therefore feed by sucking on the coral tissues.

Dove Shells *Columbellidae*

Genus *Columbella* Lamarck, 1799

Common Dove Shell *Columbella mercatoria*
½ to ¾ inch   N.E. Florida, West Indies to Brazil
These shells are brightly coloured with purple, orange, red, brown
or black dappled on white. The body whorl is solid with numerous
ridges across the shell. The aperture is narrow with a thick toothed
outer lip. The shell often has a heavy layer of coralline deposits on
its mossy periostracum, matching its feeding ground on and under
intertidal rocks, camouflaging it well and making it difficult to spot.
It is a vegetarian, feeding on algae. It is very common in beach drift.

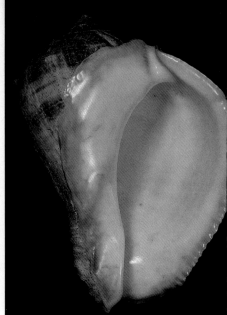

GIANT HAIRY MELONGENA,
Pugilina morio

WEST INDIAN CROWN CONCH,
Melongena melongena

Crown Conch *Melongenidae*

Crown Conchs are highly carnivorous snails, and a major species of the mud flats and mangrove swamps in their area of distribution. *Melongena melongena* is an ancient species as indicated by its abundance in quaternary fossil formations in Martinique.

Genus *Melongena* Schumacher, 1817

West Indian Crown Conch *Melongena melongena*

3 to 10 inches   Florida and West Indies

A handsome, solid species with broad dark spiral banding on a cream coloured body whorl, the base of which bears blunt spines. The aperture is highly glossed, the outer lip flaring and wavy edged. It has a thick mossy periostracum and an oval horny operculum. The animals are highly carnivorous and prey on burrowing bivalves. An inhabitant of the shallow waters of mangrove swamps and enclosed bays. The sexes are separate and females lay strings of fan shaped capsules.

Genus *Pugilina* Schumacher, 1817

Giant Hairy Melongena *Pugilina morio*
3 to 7 inches   West Africa, Guadeloupe, Martinique,
                                 Trinidad, Venezuela and Brazil
A solid spindle-shaped shell. The colour is dark chocolate, usually with a central, narrow, yellow, spiral band and knobbed whorls. The aperture is a glossy blue black. This species has a very specific distribution, being abundant only in soft mud close to mangrove roots. It is carnivorous and also a scavenger. The eggs are funnel shaped.

Nassa Mud Snails *Nassariidae*

Genus *Nassarius* Duméril, 1806

Nassa mud snails are prolific members of the intertidal and littoral zones of our shores. They have highly developed and sensitive taste and smell organs, scavenging on dead crabs, fish and invertebrates. The sexes are separate, the female laying rows of encapsulated eggs.

Common Eastern Nassa *Nassarius vibex*
½ to 1 inch   S. U.S. and West Indies
A small snail identified by its heavy glazed body shield, and beaded ribs across the shell. The body whorls are brown with paler bandings.

Variable Nassa *Nassarius albus*
½ inch   S. U.S. and West Indies
This shell is square in appearance, and may be variable in colour according to its environment from North to South. It lives lightly buried in sand and mud.

Tulip Shells *Fasciolariidae*

Genus *Fasciolaria* Lamarck 1799

True Tulip *Fasciolaria tulipa*
4 to 10 inches   S. Florida, West Indies to Brazil
A large, richly coloured shell with dark spiral bandings. The aperture is cream coloured with a lengthened siphonal canal. Species vary in colour according to environment and may be orange, red, yellow, pink, or tan. The animal is very aggressive and highly carnivorous feeding on other molluscs, it is in its turn highly edible. The frilly,

TRUE TULIP, *Fasciolaria tulipa*

BRAZILIAN SPINDLE SHELL, *Fusinus brasiliensis*

fan shaped eggs are laid in masses, and unfertilised eggs are known to serve as food for developing embryos. It lives from the intertidal zone on sand, mud and coral to depths of 8 fathoms.

Spindles and Latirus *Fusinus*

This is a family of attractive, heavy shells often with long siphonal canals. Most live in shallow mud sediment where they feed on other invertebrates.

Genus *Fusinus* Rafinesque 1815

Brazilian Spindle Shell *Fusinus brasiliensis*

4 to 7 inches   S. Caribbean and Brazil

A white spindle shaped shell, with 8 or 9 angular body whorls. It has numerous spiral cords stained brown or orange and a long siphonal canal. The animal has a sickle shaped operculum. It lives on sand and mud bottoms, where it feeds on worms and other small invertebrates at depths of 2 to 10 fathoms.

BROWN-LINED LATIRUS, *Latirus infundibulum*

Genus *Latirus* Montfort 1810

Brown Lined Latirus   *Latirus infundibulum*

2 to 4 inches   Florida Keys to West Indies

A spindle shaped shell with a short siphonal canal. The colour may be cream to chocolate-brown with numerous darker heavy spiral cords. The aperture has 3 or 4 folds, and is highly glossed and creamy. The animal has a sickle shaped operculum, and velvety outer coating. It favours mud and estuarine conditions from depths of 1 to 15 fathoms.

Genus *Leucozonia* Gray 1847

Chestnut Latirus   *Leucozonia nassa*

1½ to 2 inches   Florida, West Indies to Brazil

The shell is yellow to dark brown with blunt spines on the body whorls, the last of which has a white or yellow band ending with a single tooth on the outer lip. The aperture is glossy white or yellow. The animal is red with a sickle shape operculum. It is common on shoreline rocks. The eggs are pink and laid in white funnels, which may often be seen on the underside of rubble. *Leucozonia nassa leucozonalis* is a smooth shouldered version of the above.

CHESTNUT LATIRUS, *Leucozonia nassa*

Vase Shells   *Turbinellidae*

There are three Vase Shells in the Caribbean, as rare in some areas
as they are common in others due to the limited range of their
habitats; as their name indicates they favour mud and are often found
in colonies.

Genus *Vasum* Röding 1798

Caribbean Vase Shell   *Vasum muricatum*

2 to 4 inches   S. Florida and West Indies

A large, heavy species with white ribbing across the shell, hidden by
a thick mossy green periostracum making it difficult to observe live.
The apertures are bright mauve with five folds; the colour fades in
dead shells. The animal has a thick sickle shaped operculum.

It is extremely rare south of Martinique, where dead specimens
were collected from Amerindian shell mounds. Its range is restricted
to the Northern Caribbean, where it lives on eel grass beds from
depths of 1 to 4 fathoms.

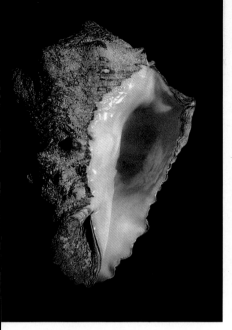

CARIBBEAN VASE SHELL, *Vasum muricatum*

SPINY VASE SHELL, *Vasum capitellum*

Spiny Vase Shell   *Vasum capitellum*

2 to 3 inches   Puerto Rico to Brazil

This species is more elongate than *V. muricatum* with prominent spines and ridges across the shell. The creamy coloured body whorls are covered by a dark brown periostracum or very often heavy encrustations. It is most common on shallow coral reefs in the central part of its geographical range, and deeper mud and sandy bottoms to depths of 10 fathoms.

Olives   *Olividae*

The shiny sand burrowing Olive shells live close to the shore or on submerged sand banks to depths of 5 fathoms. They are mostly active at night or during tidal change. Their sizeable mantles protect the polished surfaces and as with Cowrie shells, their internal skeletons become absorbed with age. Close inspection reveals that their shells have an underlayer with a different pattern and colour to the final, outer one. The animal is skilled at overlaying a damaged shell with fresh enamel.

As carnivores preying on crabs, shrimps, other molluscs and small fish, they plough through the sand leaving deep troughs and only their

NETTED OLIVE, *Oliva reticularis*   CARIBBEAN OLIVE SHELL, *Oliva scripta*

long inhalant siphon showing. They have been seen capturing small flounders, which they smother and enfold with their fleshy foot, burrowing into the sand with their prey to devour them, often accompanied by other olives. Olive shells are the only marine molluscs to lay free unattached egg capsules, which are rolled about by waves and tidal movements to keep them oxygenated and healthy.

Genus *Oliva* Bruguière 1798

Netted Olive   *Oliva reticularis*
1 to 2 inches   S.E. Florida, West Indies, Venezuela
This species is white or cream coloured with brown or mauve triangular markings which are variable according to environment. Rare albinos, yellow and black specimens have been recorded.

Caribbean Olive Shell   *Oliva scripta*
2 to 2½ inches   N. Carolina, West Indies, Brazil
A large olive shell with deeply channelled apical whorls. The colour is cream, grey and tan with very variable patterns, either triangles, dashes, lines or spots, and occasionally banding. Albinos and all-black colouration exists. The animals live in colonies.

BEADED MITRE, *Mitra nodulosa*

WHITE LINED MITRE, *Pusia albocincta*

Mitres *Mitridae*

Genus *Mitra* Lamarck 1799

Beaded Mitre *Mitra nodulosa*

½ to 1½ inches   Florida, West Indies

A spindle shaped shell with a narrow aperture and 4 white stained folds. The body whorls are brown or yellow with numerous rows of fine beads. It lives in shallow water in mud and under rocks, where it preys on small clams and worms.

Genus *Pusia* Swainson 1840

White Lined Mitre *Pusia albocincta*

1 inch   Florida, West Indies

A handsome, shiny, black shell with numerous ribs across the width of the shell decorated with distinctive spiral lines which have a white diamond shaped patterning. The aperture is purple with paler coloured folds. The animal is highly carnivorous with a long retractable snout. It lives in coral sand at depths from 1 to 12 fathoms.

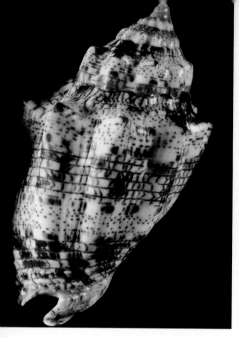

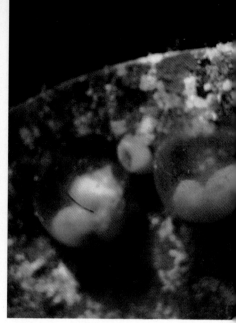

MUSIC VOLUTE, *Voluta musica*

MUSIC VOLUTE, *Voluta musica*, egg cases

Volutes *Volutidae*

Two true Volutes live in the Caribbean; the Music Volute is a common West Indian species. The Hebrew Volute is rare in Caribbean waters other than off the shores of Venezuela and Brazil.

Genus *Voluta* Linné 1758

Music Volute *Voluta musica*

2 to 4½ inches   West Indies

The Music Volute is one of the rare members of the genus to have an operculum. The heavy shell has intricate patterns resembling written music which is repeated on the animal's mantle. The shells are variable in colour according to their environment, which may be sand, coral and eel grass of the intertidal zone, to the deeper reefs of 15 fathoms. The outer lip is smooth with strong black markings. The sexes are separate with reproduction taking place in Spring and Summer. Miniature volutes are laid in capsules often attached to the inside of dead bivalves. The capsule has a weak crescent in the centre to help the young shell to escape. Highly carnivorous from birth, they prey on other molluscs which they paralyse with a purple dye-stained

COMMON NUTMEG, *Cancellaria reticulata*

mucus. It is not unusual to see Music Volutes active during the day although they are generally nocturnal.

Genus *Cancellaria* Lamarck 1799

Common Nutmeg   *Cancellaria reticulata*
1 to 2½ inches   S.E. U.S. and West Indies to Brazil
A heavy, oval shell with strong spiral cords and growth lines which create a crosshatched appearance. The aperture is glossy with 3 folds, the outer lip is heavily ridged. The body colouring is white with orange banding, usually hidden by a dark brown velvety periostracum. The Common Nutmeg favours mud bottoms at depths from 3 to 12 fathoms, where it feeds on other invertebrates.

Cones   *Conidae*
The rarest molluscs in the world are Cones. For the collector, these beautiful shells with multiple colours and patterns, and the many subtle variations in shape caused by environment and diet are puzzling; the only sure way to identify such shells is by examining the tongue (or radula).

A closer look at these remarkable molluscs reveals an extraordinary

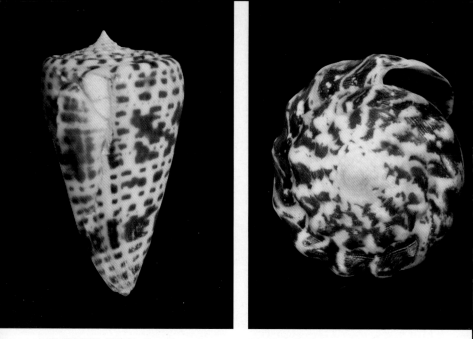

ALPHABET CONE, *Conus spurius atlanticus*

CROWN CONE, *Conus regius*, (spire)

stock of venomous single teeth or harpoons. A two lobed sac is hidden behind the animal's snout; the upper lobe has individual, hardened, hollow, arrow like teeth, the lower lobe contains many more in the process of hardening. From this double reservoir a long string-like tube leads to a pear shaped gland which stores a toxic liquid produced by the digestive system. When the Cone has located its prey and is ready to attack, this liquid runs through the tube and fills the hollow tooth waiting in the top lobe. The weapon is shot through the water by the mollusc and the unsuspecting prey is immediately paralysed by the poison. The cone then draws its prey into its expanded snout and a fresh tooth immediately replaces the old one.

In the Caribbean, Crown and Alphabet Cones are known to inflict minor stings and so they should be handled carefully and held by their base. Breeding takes place in the summer, the females often remain to protect their spawn. Cones frequently cannibalise their own species.

Genus *Conus* Linné 1758

Alphabet Cone *Conus spurius atlanticus*
2 to 3 inches   Florida, West Indies to Brazil
A handsome glossy species with either orange or brown bands or

MOUSE CONE, *Conus mus*

dashes on a white background. It lives beneath the sand to depths of 10 fathoms. Dead shells are common during port dredging operations.

Crown Cone   *Conus regius*
1½ to 3 inches   S.E. Florida, West Indies to Brazil
The commonest of the West Indian Cone shells with distinctive knobbed shoulders. The body whorl is beaded with chocolate mottling on white, or all yellow with white. The spires are often heavily encrusted and the shell has a thin periostracum. The animal is coloured scarlet. It lives in coral sand and crevices near reefs from the shoreline to a depth of 12 fathoms.

Mouse Cone   *Conus mus*
1 to 1½ inches   S.E. Florida, West Indies
An olive coloured shell with numerous spiral ridges and a mossy periostracum. The inner lip is coloured deep mauve. Beach specimens are bright pink. It lives intertidally, under rocks in soft sand or mud, to depths of 12 fathoms where it hides in crevices.

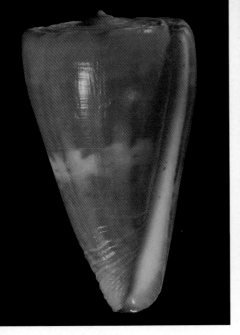 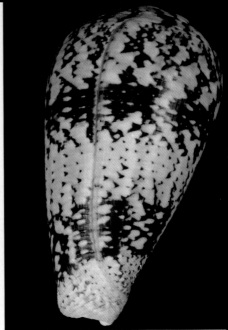

CARROT CONE, *Conus daucus*   TURTLE CONE, *Conus ermineus*

Carrot Cone   *Conus daucus*

1½ to 2½ inches   Florida, West Indies to Venezuela

A low spired cone usually with a glossy red body whorl decorated with a central band of brown dots or white areas. Hybrid specimens may be mauve, yellow or albinos. A thin, ridged periostracum is often present, together with thick encrustations. The aperture is bright mauve in live specimens, fading in dead shells. Shells are frequently cast ashore. It lives in shallow reef areas beneath rocks and on coral sand to depths of 12 fathoms.

Turtle Cone   *Conus ermineus*

2 to 4 inches   West Africa, Caribbean to Brazil

A distinctive round shouldered cone shell. The body whorl is grey-blue or white with brown or purple mottling or bands, overlaid with dashes. Some species are red and pink, when the normal dark brown outer covering is orange. It lives in coral sand under rocks, occasionally in the mud of shallow eel grass beds, from the shoreline to depths of 12 fathoms.

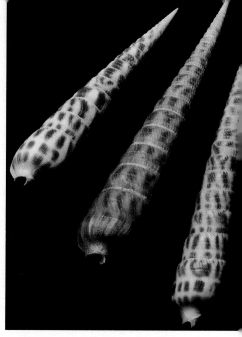

ANTILLEAN CONE, *Conus cedo nulli* FLAME AUGER, *Terebra taurinus*

Antillean Cone *Conus cedo nulli*
2 to 3 inches   Lesser Antilles to Brazil
This cone is included for the sake of conservation of a rare species.
Its habitat was badly abused by commercial shell dealers during its
breeding seasons, one such harvest is illustrated; the species
ultimately disappeared from many areas in the Southern Caribbean
in 1980. Divers are now asked to protect the small remaining colonies
of this beautiful shell and allow it to continue to breed.

Turrets and Augers *Terebridae, Turridae*

Genus *Terebra* Bruguière, 1789

Flame Auger *Terebra taurinus*
4 to 6 inches   S.E. Florida, West Indies to Brazil
Although rare, this long narrow auger is occasionally found in
estuaries. The shell has numerous body whorls with bown zigzag
markings. The animals are carnivorous with sickle shaped
operculums. They live to depths of 15 fathoms on soft mud bottoms.

Bubble Shells *Bullidae*

Genus *Bulla* Linné 1758

Striated Bubble *Bulla striata*
1 to 1½ inches   W. Florida, West Indies to Venezuela

A bulbous shell with a smooth brown mottled body whorl; the base has a distinctive small hole near the top. The animal is grey brown, with its mantle covering most of the shell. It lives in sand and mud of shallow eel grass; although the dead shells of this species litter such areas, they are nocturnal and will only be seen in large numbers when they emerge to feed.

Pyram *Pyramidellidae*

Genus *Pyramidella* Lamarck 1799

Giant Atlantic Pyrum *Pyramidella dolabrata*
1 to 1½ inches   West Indies

A highly polished species. The body whorls are creamy white with brown spiral lines. The internal column has strong folds in adults. The animal is a member of the *opistobranchia* family and lacks a tongue, it feeds mainly on worms. It lives in sand and eel grass to depths of 8 fathoms.

STRIATED BUBBLE, *Bulla striata*   GIANT ATLANTIC PYRUM,
                                          Pyramidella dolabrata

Clams, scallops and mussels — the bivalves

Bivalves *Pelecypoda* or *Lamellibranchia*

Cockles and clams have been and are of great importance to the human economy, but in many cases their existence has become threatened by pollution and overcollection.

Their use by Amerindians and prehistoric peoples of the Caribbean was varied, complex and imaginative and these shells were to contribute largely to the survival of the seaborn migrating populations of the Orinoco and Amazon delta regions more than 2000 years ago. The hardy and excellent Carib Indian divers, who, under Spanish rule were made to harvest the Atlantic Pearl Oyster, *Pinctada radiata*, from the sea beds off the islands of Coche, Cubagua and Margarita. They left behind them mountains of lustrous mother-of-pearl, one in every 40 of these shells contained an irregular pearl. The Indians marked out strange, vast playing courts with the discarded valves. The heart shaped cockles were believed to have been tools of spirits, used for scraping and cleaning the impure souls of the deceased, and never eaten for fear of death.

Legion are the myths surrounding the bivalve shell. Many of the shells illustrated are remarkably beautiful, others are well known food sources.

Ark Clams *Arcidae*

Genus *Arca* Linné 1758

Turkey Wing *Arca zebra*
2 to 4 inches   N. Carolina, West Indies to Brazil
A solid, ribbed bivalve with brown-red zigzag markings. It lives attached to rocks and on coarse sand bottoms in shallow water. It attaches itself by a mass of strong threads which it secretes, called byssus. The blood red animal is a favourite bait for fishermen. Although the meat of this clam has a bitter taste it has been used for many centuries to make soup and chowder.

Mossy Ark *Arca imbricata*
1 to 3 inches   N. Carolina and West Indies
The valves are chalky white and ribbed, with a very thick periostracum and leaf-like outer edges, giving the shell a winged

TURKEY WING, *Arca zebra*

MOSSY ARK, *Arca imbricata*   EARED ARK, *Anadara notabilis*

appearance. The shell is often encased by the rock it is attached to. It lives submerged to depths of 10 fathoms on and near coral reef formations.

Genus *Anadara* Deshayes 1830

Eared Ark   *Anadara notabilis*

2 to 4 inches   Florida, West Indies to Brazil

A heavy, rotund, white bivalve with pink stains on the hooked prominence at the apex of each half of the shell (the umbones). 26-28 parallel ribs are crossed by numerous concentric threads. The valve margins are interlocking. The valve interiors are often stained green. The shell has a thick brown matted periostracum. It lives on mud and grass bottoms from depths of 1 foot to 4 fathoms.

Bittersweets   *Glycymeridae*

Genus *Glycymeris* da Costa 1778

Decussate Bittersweet   *Glycymeris decussata*

2 to 2½ inches   S.E. Florida, West Indies to Brazil

A heavy, inflated shell, round in appearance with a curved hinge. The

DECUSSATE BITTERSWEET
Glycymeris decussata

COMB BITTERSWEET, *Glycymeris pectinata* (bottom) and ATLANTIC BITTERSWEET, *Glycymeris undata* (top)

The colour is greyish white with chestnut splotches, it may also be uniformly white or brown. The sculpture consists of numerous radiating lines and the shell has only a thin periostracum. This is an ancient family evolving from Jurassic times. They burrow in sand and live at depths from 1 to 100 fathoms.

Comb Bittersweet *Glycymeris pectinata*
½ to 1 inch   S.E. U.S., West Indies to Brazil
Oval, chalky white valves with brown or pink mottling of the strong, radiating ribs. It lives in sand on shallow reefs.

Atlantic Bittersweet *Glycymeris undata*
2 inches   S.E. U.S., West Indies
This shell resembles *G. decussata*, but its valves are more regular in shape and the beaks are more centrally placed. The radiating ribs are cream or white with tan mottling. It lives in the sand to a depth of 10 fathoms.

YELLOW MUSSEL, *Brachidontes citrinus* (left) and SCORCHED MUSSEL, *Brachidontes exustus* (right)

Mussels *Mytilidae*

This family is famous for its edible quality, and has colonised many intertidal areas of the world's oceans. Those of the West Indies cover most of its ancient reef formation, but are small and of little nourishment to humans. All mussels are attached by a mass of silky byssal threads and have frilly mantle edges. They are filter feeders.

The mussel *Mytilus edulis platensis* lives near estuaries in the Southern Caribbean, often attached to submerged rocks. It has been the cause of death during the rainy season, when what are known as "red tides" or "mar rojo" occur. These tides are caused by the flooding of low lying areas, the following rise in water temperature allows a poisonous form of red plankton to multiply and increase in toxicity. The mussel filters and feeds on this plankton, and no amount of cooking can subsequently destroy the poison. This season lasts from August to November, at which time the mussels must be avoided. However when tides are normal these mussels are one of the best foods of the South American mainland, and are eaten smoked, boiled and stuffed.

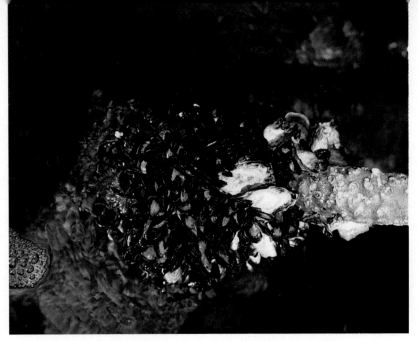

HOOKED MUSSEL, *Brachidontes recurvus* and CARIBBEAN OYSTER, *Crassostrea rhizophorae*

Genus *Brachidontes* Swainson, 1840

Yellow Mussel *Brachidontes citrinus*
1 to 1½ inches   S.E. Florida, West Indies
Silver-purple valves, with stained umbones and numerous radiating ribs. The hinge has 30 very small teeth. It lives in colonies on intertidal reefs and rocks.

Scorched Mussel *Brachidontes exustus*
¾ inch   Florida and West Indies
A smaller and more sharply angled mussel with brown-yellow valves tinged with mauve. The interior is purple-white. It lives in colonies with *B. citrinus*.

Hooked Mussel *Brachidontes recurvus*
1 to 2 inches   S.E. U.S., West Indies
The valves of this mussel are distinctively triangular and obliquely curved. Its shell is strongly ribbed and a blue-black colour with a rosy-brown interior. It lives in clusters on intertidal rocks and pilings.

FLAT TREE OYSTER, *Isognomon alatus*

ATLANTIC WING OYSTER, *Pteria colymbus*

Oysters   *Isognomonidae*

Genus *Isognomon* Solander 1786

Flat Tree Oyster   *Isognomon alatus*

3 to 4 inches   S. Florida, West Indies to Brazil

A flat, purple coloured shell with straight grooved hinges. The interior of the valves is pearly. The shell is distinctively fan-shaped. It lives on mangrove roots and pilings in large, communal clusters. Although edible it is poorly flavoured.

Genus *Pteria* Scopoli 1777

Atlantic Wing Oyster   *Pteria colymbus*

1½ to 4 inches   S.E. U.S. and West Indies

This shell has a characteristic extension of the posterior wing which gives the open bivalve the appearance of a silhouette of a bird in flight. The valves are externally brown-black with dark brown radial lines. The interiors are a beautiful mother-of-pearl. These animals live as parasites on soft corals in water to depths of 4 fathoms. It is this shell that was used for the manufacture of the exquisite pendants by the Guapoid and Saladoid Indians more than 2000 years ago.

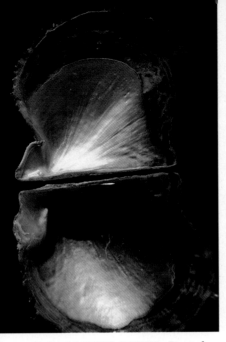 

ATLANTIC PEARL OYSTER, *Pinctada radiata*

CARIBBEAN OYSTER, *Crassostrea rhizophorae*

Genus *Pinctada* Röding 1798

Atlantic Pearl Oyster *Pinctada radiata*

2 to 4 inches   S.E. Florida, West Indies to Venezuela

A fragile, delicate bivalve with overlapping frilled scales of green and gold. The interior of the valves are mother-of-pearl. The mantle may contain an irregular pearl. It lives in clusters and attaches itself by strong, slender threads to rocks and hard coral. It may also live individually, from the intertidal zone to a depth of 3 fathoms. These oysters are edible but not very palatable. The valves were used to make jewellery by the Carib and Arawak Indians of the Antilles.

Genus *Crassostrea* Sacco 1897

Caribbean Oyster *Crassostrea rhizophorae*

2 to 5 inches   Caribbean, Venezuela, Brazil

This is the tasty, edible Caribbean Oyster, which lives attached in colonies to the roots of mangroves. Those living in the colder waters of the Caribbean are usually larger and better tasting. In the Antilles reintroduction is being attempted in many swamp areas. This is more or less successful according to the salinity and oxygen renewal of the

81

COON OYSTER, *Ostrea frons*

water, and the health of the mangrove itself. The shell varies in shape according to its support, although the upper valve as in true oysters is flat, fitting deep into the lower one. They are silver coloured with faint purple mottling.

Genus *Ostrea* Linné 1758

Coon Oyster *Ostrea frons*
1 to 2½ inches   S.E. U.S. and West Indies
The valves of this oyster are purple, red, brown or gold with brilliant mother-of-pearl interiors which are pimpled around the margin edges. The valves are long and narrow with wavy edges. The animal lives in shallow coral reefs, attached to sea whips and other soft corals, hanging on by virtue of their unique clasping projections, situated on the lower valve. The shells are frequently cast ashore.

AMBER PEN SHELL, *Pinna carnea*

Pen Shells   *Pinnidae*

Genus *Pinna* Linné 1758

Amber Pen Shell   *Pinna carnea*

6 to 8 inches   S.E. Florida to West Indies

A unique family of tall fragile fan shaped bivalves. They stand upright, firmly attached to the sediment by a clump of solid byssal threads mixed with rough sand and detritus. The valves are usually pale pink with orange interiors. The sculpturing consists of 8 to 12 radial ribs which are either smooth or decorated with flute like spines. A minute crab lives in the mantle as a commensal feeder. Well organised, the *Pinna* discards unwanted debris via its waste canal. It lives in shallow subtidal areas on eel grass and sand bottoms.

ZIGZAG SCALLOP, *Pecten ziczac*   SENTIS SCALLOP, *Chlamys sentis*

Scallops *Pectinidae*

Genus *Pecten* Müller 1776

Zigzag Scallop *Pecten ziczac*

2 to 4 inches   S.E. U.S., West Indies to Brazil

The upper flat valve of this scallop is brilliantly coloured; the broad, low ribs are mottled with pink, brown, and white. The lower, inflated valve has less marked ribbing and is uniformly white. The animal lives in shallow eel grass, just beneath the sand with its numerous eyes and tentacles outlining the shell margins. The scallop is often attracted to submerged wrecks and pilings. An excellent food clam.

Genus *Chlamys* Röding 1798

Sentis Scallop *Chlamys sentis*

1½ inches   Carolina, West Indies to Brazil

A flat valved clam, with 40 to 50 rough thin ribs. The "ears" on the hinges are not equal. Coloured tan, orange, red and white. Lives attached to the underside of submerged rocks and corals to a depth of 6 fathoms. The scallop illustrated had digested a baby triton.

84

LION'S PAW SCALLOP, *Lyropecten nodosus*

CALICO SCALLOP, *Aequipecten gibbus*

Genus *Lyropecten* Conrad 1862

Lion's Paw Scallop   *Lyropecten nodosus*
3 to 7 inches   S.E. U.S., West Indies to Venezuela
A large beautiful scallop, with strongly knobbed ribs and brilliant
jewel colours of red, orange and yellow. Only single valves are
common on beaches; the living animal favours soft mud and sand
from depths of 4 to 30 fathoms.

Genus *Aequipecten* P. Fischer 1886

Calico Scallop   *Aequipecten gibbus*
1 to 2 inches   E. U.S., West Indies to Brazil
A solid, round clam shell with 20 well defined squarish ribs. The
valves are white, mottled with irregular zigzag markings of brown
and pink. It is common in shallow eel grass beds and mangrove
environments.

85

ATLANTIC THORNY OYSTER,
Spondylus americanus

DIGITATE THORNY OYSTER,
Spondylus ictericus

Thorny Oysters *Spondylidae*

Genus *Spondylus* Linné 1758

Atlantic Thorny Oyster *Spondylus americanus*

3 to 8 inches   Florida, West Indies to Venezuela

This is the most exquisite bivalve shell in the West Indies. It is the deep water specimens living in undisturbed conditions that secrete the beautiful long spines and leaf-like additions to the lower valve. In this environment they live in colonies. Shallow water *spondylus* have the same shaped valves, but only a few, blunt spines. The valves have a typical ball and socket hinge with glossy white interiors; one muscle scar is present on the lower valve. The spines often attract coralline deposits and may be camouflaged by sponge. The shell colour is mainly white, scarlet, orange and pink.

Digitate Thorny Oyster *Spondylus ictericus*

2 to 3 inches   S.E. Florida, West Indies to Brazil

The valves of this shell are bright red or mauve with white mottling. Its spines are blunt and finger-like at the ends. They live attached to submerged debris, shallow rocks and rubble on sand bottoms.

File Shells *Limidae*

Genus *Lima* Bruguière, 1796

Rough Lima *Lima scabra*

1 to 4 inches   S.E. Florida and West Indies

All three members of the *Lima* family in the Caribbean have the most extravagant mantles of all the bivalves. Either pink, white or scarlet tentacles more than the length of the shell itself decorate the mantle margin, which is scarlet in the case of *Lima scabra*. The white valves are strongly sculptured by radiating ribs, covered by a tough, brown periostracum. The animal is normally attached by a mass of silky green byssal threads but can disengage itself immediately when disturbed, swimming clumsily with jerking movements in search of more reliable quarters. These are spectacular shells in an aquarium. *Lima* live submerged in deep marine crevices and under ledges. The small, fragile *L. pellucida* lives attached to the underside of rocks.

ROUGH LIMA, *Lima scabra*

PENNSYLVANIA LUCINE, *Lucina pensylvanica*

Lucine Clams *Lucinidae*

Genus *Lucina* Bruguière 1797

Pennsylvania Lucine   *Lucina pensylvanica*

2 inches   Florida, West Indies

This is the much sought after "palourde" placed so highly on the list in French West Indian cuisine. It is very often dug out by foot, as a family activity at Christmas and Easter. The animal lives in shallow sand depressions in company with the sea cucumber *Holothuria cubana*. The shells are heavily ridged and glossy white with a straw coloured periostracum. The margins are stained orange in some areas. Their excellent edible quality is probably due to the long worm shaped foot which manufactures a sandy tube through which it filters, cleans, feeds and rejects debris. Beach specimens are completely smooth.

TIGER LUCINA, *Codakia orbicularis*

LEAFY JEWEL BOX, *Chama macerophylla*

Genus *Codakia* Scopoli 1777

Tiger Lucine   *Codakia orbicularis*

2 to 3 inches   Florida, West Indies to Brazil

The valves are off-white, circular and semi-inflated with a network of sculpturing. The margins are deep pink. The animal burrows in submerged sand and is found at depths down to 20 fathoms. It is one of the commonest bivalve shells to be cast ashore in the West Indies.

Jewel Boxes   *Chamidae*

Genus *Chama* Linné, 1758

Leafy Jewel Box   *Chama macerophylla*

1 to 3 inches   N. Carolina, Florida, West Indies to Brazil

These are vividly coloured shells of lavender, yellow, pink, brick red or white, with waves of leafy spines thickly decorating the outer valves. The raised areas on each valve near the hinge (the umbones) are frequently tinted yellow. It lives permanently attached to rocks and coral rubble from depths of a foot to 12 fathoms; rare unattached specimens live in deep water.

TRUE SPINY JEWEL BOX,
Echinochama arcinella, parasite to
Strombus pugilis

MAGNUM COCKLE, *Trachycardium
magnum*

Genus *Echinochama* P. Fischer 1887

True Spiny Jewel Box   *Echinochama arcinella*

1 to 2 inches   West Indies to Brazil

Usually white or pink with numerous rows of blunt, spiny, radial
ribs. The valves are curved, and the lunule heart shaped. It is freeliving
in soft mud and sand from depths of 2 to 15 fathoms. Shallow water
specimens are often attached to hard surfaces.

Cockles   *Cardiidae*

Genus *Trachycardium* Mörch 1853

Magnum Cockle   *Trachycardium magnum*

2 to 4 inches   S. Florida, West Indies, Venezuela

A glossy pink or yellow, smooth ribbed, heart shaped shell. The 30
to 35 ribs are scaled. The animal lives in clear coral sand at depths
from 1 to 15 fathoms. It is locally common in certain areas of the
Southern Caribbean.

90

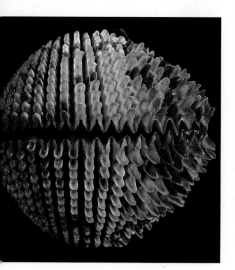

PRICKLY COCKLE, *Trachycardium isocardia*

COMMON EGG COCKLE, *Laevicardium laevigatum*

West Indies Prickly Cockle   *Trachycardium isocardia*
2 to 4 inches   West Indies and Venezuela
This is a very beautiful cockle; the inflated valves are mottled with grey and pink, and have some 35 radial ribs with numerous overlapping flute like scales. It lives in eel grass and shallow reef conditions, it is often found in colonies.

Genus *Laevicardium* Swainson 1840

Common Egg Cockle   *Laevicardium laevigatum*
1 to 2 inches   West Indies and Venezuela
The valves are highly polished, inflated and bright yellow, often stained with pink or brown flecks and concentric lines. The interiors are white. It is very common submerged in sand to a depth of 6 fathoms.

91

SPINY PAPER COCKLE, *Papyridea soleniformis*

PRINCESS VENUS, *Antigona listeri*

Genus *Papyridea* Swainson 1840

Spiny Paper Cockle *Papyridea soleniformis*

1 to 2 inches   S.E. U.S., West Indies, Venezuela

The shell is fragile and gaping, the valves are pink or orange splashed with darker colours. There are 50 to 55 fine, oblique, radial ribs which have minute spines at their edges. It lives in moderately shallow water in sand, from depths of 1 ft to 10 fathoms.

Venus Clams *Veneridae*

Genus *Antigona* Schumacher 1817

Princess Venus *Antigona listeri*

2 to 4 inches   S.E. Florida and West Indies

This bivalve is a favourite food of the Slipper Lobster. The shell is cream coloured with pale brown streaks. The valves have numerous tiny radial riblets and pronounced concentric upturned ridges. The valve interiors are white and glossy with deep purple stains. It lives in sand to depths of 8 fathoms.

KING VENUS, *Chione paphia*

TRIGONAL TIVELA, *Tivela mactroides*

Genus *Chione* Mühlfeld 1811

King Venus *Chione paphia*

1 to 1½ inches   L. Florida Keys, West Indies to Brazil

The white valves have 7 to 9 upturned concentric ridges towards the hinge, which are mottled with brown or purple. There is a distinct bulge on the margin towards the hinge which gives the shell a heart-shaped outline. It lives buried in sand from depths of 1 to 20 fathoms.

Genus *Tivela* Link 1807

Trigonal Tivela *Tivela mactroides*

1 to 2 inches   West Indies to Brazil

A shiny solid bivalve with broad rays of brown and white, or uniformly chestnut. The inner valves are glossy white. A favourite food shell for Venezuelans, it is fished below the tide line by foot. It is also frequently found in Amerindian shell mounds, where it was pierced and used as a pendant, or to make necklaces.

93

CALICO CLAM, *Macrocallista maculata*

SUNRISE TELLIN, *Tellina radiata*

Genus *Macrocallista* Meek 1876

Calico Clam *Macrocallista maculata*

1½ to 4 inches   S.E. U.S., West Indies to Brazil

A coffee coloured glossy oval bivalve with a chequered pattern, often hidden beneath a thin brown periostracum. The interior is glossy white. It lives in submerged coral sand and mud to depths of 10 fathoms.

Tellins   *Tellinidae*

Genus *Tellina* Linné 1758

Tellins are beautiful, long, thin, highly glossed shells, with richly coloured valves. They are burrowers, living in clear coral sand from the intertidal zone to 20 fathoms or more. Most prefer areas where there is a steady renewal of oxygen. They have two separate siphons with which they filter particles sucked in from the surface above them. Each species has a very specific muscle scar and ligaments which are external.

Sunrise Tellin   *Tellina radiata*
1½ to 4 inches   S.E. U.S. and West Indies
The valves have wide pink rays on yellow or white. The umbones
(the raised areas on the two valves, close to the hinge) are stained
red. A pure white subspecies exists known as *T. radiata unimaculata.*
The species lives in shallow sand.

Speckled Tellin   *Tellina listeri*
2 to 4 inches   S.E. U.S. and West Indies
The valves are rough, coloured cream with brown speckles and the
interiors are glossy yellow. The outside of the shell is sculptured with
numerous concentric threads. Rare specimens are coloured white and
purple. It lives in sand from depths of 3 feet to 20 fathoms.

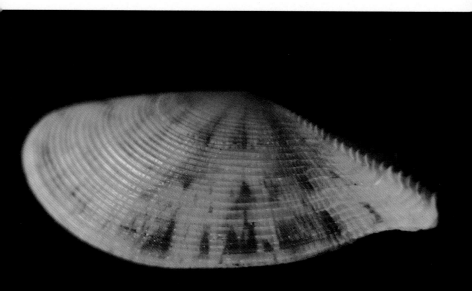

SPECKLED TELLIN, *Tellina listeri*

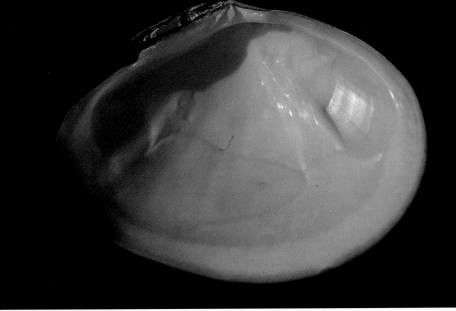

FAUST TELLIN, *Arcopagia fausta*

Genus *Arcopagia* Brown 1827

Faust Tellin *Arcopagia fausta*
2 to 4 inches   Florida and West Indies
A solid chalky shell with a yellow stained glossy interior. The
ligament on the hinge is very prominent and the shell retains the
tough periostracum around its margin edges. A very common bivalve
living in sand to a depth of 10 fathoms. It is the favourite food of
Octopus vulgaris; as many as 150 empty shells have been counted,
neatly piled up at the entrance to such a den.

Genus *Strigilla* Turton 1822

Large Strigilla *Strigilla carnaria*
¾ to 1 inch   S.E. U.S. and West Indies
A totally pink tellin with numerous radial lines which are rather
disorganised. Living in sandy areas beneath the waves, it is a favourite
prey of *Natica* as seen by the many perforated shells illustrated.

LARGE STRIGILLA, *Strigilla carnaria*

COMMON CARIBBEAN DONAX,
Donax denticulatus

Donaxes *Donacidae*

Genus *Donax* Linné 1758

Common Caribbean Donax *Donax denticulata*

1 inch   West Indies, Venezuela

A shiny wedge shaped clam, extremely variable in colour and pattern. It may be uniformly pink, white, mauve, yellow or purple, or white with bold rays. Fishing this delicious shell has been a favourite pastime for fishermen for more than 2000 years in the Caribbean. The *donax* living in massive colonies just beneath the sand may be caught as the waves retreat. In Venezuela, it is a common sight to see children taking home buckets full of the little clam which their mothers make into excellent soup. Despite their nomadic habits, *donax* are also a favourite food of other snails, crabs and wading birds, who are always aware of their movements.

Sanguins *Sanguinolariidae*

Genus *Asaphis* Modeer 1793

Gaudy Asaphis *Asaphis deflorata*
1½ to 3 inches   S.E. Florida and West Indies
A brightly coloured wrinkled shell, either pink, yellow or lavender.
The interior of the valves are glossy with deeper tones. The shell is
sculptured by numerous concentric threads and radial lines. It lives
in the coarse sand of semi-enclosed bays, and close to mangroves.
It is yet another favourite shell food in the French islands, where it
is eaten stuffed.

Razor Clams *Solenidae*

Genus *Solen* Linné 1758

Antillean Jack-knife Clam *Solen obliquus*
4 to 6 inches   West Indies
Razor clams are well known on the mud flats of Europe. In the
Caribbean they live submerged in the mud and sand of shallow reefs
and eel grass beds. The long valves are strong in adults but fragile
in immature specimens. A thick periostracum hides faint pink or
brown rays which decorate both of the white valves. The animal is
able to jump about by pumping strong jets of water through its
siphons.

GAUDY ASAPHIS, *Asaphis deflorata*   ANTILLEAN JACKNIFE CLAM, *Solen obliquus*

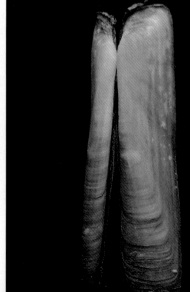

CAMPECHE ANGEL WING, *Pholas campechiensis*

Angel Wings   *Pholadidae*

The shells of this family are extraordinarily beautiful but equally as dangerous and destructive in their role as ill reputed wood borers, causing severe damage to buildings and docks along sea borders and even to ships themselves. With their solid, gaping, reinforced foreward margins and a special secretion, they are able to bore into cement, rock and wood. The species illustrated is known to confine its activities to burrowing into deep mud and is rarely found to be a nuisance.

Genus *Pholas* Linné 1758

Campeche Angel Wing   *Pholas campechiensis*
3 to 4 inches   N. Carolina, West Indies to Brazil
The chalky white valves are long and thin with well developed bead-like radiating ribs and numerous concentric threads. There is a rolled umbone near the hinge supported by 12 smaller shelly plates, unique to this genus. The animal has a strong, long, ridged siphon used for burrowing. The soft body is attached to cup like projections placed beneath the hinge region. Angel Wings live in moderately shallow waters in quiet bays.

Glossary of shell terms

Most words used in this shell book may be found in a good dictionary. The specialised terms used to describe the anatomical parts of molluscs are found in advanced identification books. The terms listed here frequently occur in shell books and have a special connotation in conchology.

adult form: fully grown; sexually mature.

albino form: all white in shell or soft parts.

aperture: opening or "mouth" of a snail shell.

apex: the beginning, smaller whorls in the upper (or posterior) end of a gastropod shell.

author: name of the person who described the taxonomic unit (family, genus, species or subspecies). The author's name is followed by the date of publication, e.g.: *Conus mus* Hwass, 1792.

axial: around or along an axis, such as longitudinal ribs of colour bands on the whorls of gastropods.

benthal: living in the ocean at depths exceeding 10,000 feet.

bivalve: member of the class Bivalvia or Pelecypoda; a clam, oyster or cockle shell.

body whorl: the largest whorl of a univalve shell.

byssus: a mass of strong threads secreted by a marine mollusc that attaches the animal to a hard, fixed surface.

carrion: rotting flesh of marine animals often consumed by *Murex* shells.

columella: the central internal spiral column of a gastropod shell.

commensal: two different marine species, such as a mollusc with shrimps or small fish, who live together without parasitic intention.

conch: a large gastropod marine shell, such as a triton shell. *Strombus, Turbinella, Fasciolaria,* etc.

conchology: the study of molluscs, usually, but not necessarily, confined to the shell.

crab specimen: a shell, usually in poor condition, formerly used as a home for a hermit crab. The columella may have a U-shaped worn area.

dextral form: a gastropod shell coiling clockwise (when viewed towards the apex); "right-handed".

diameter: greatest width of a snail shell at right angles to the shell axis.

dimorphism: condition of a species having two different inherited, morphological forms, such as males being smaller or of different colouration (sexual dimorphism) than the females.

ecologic form: a morphological condition brought about by the influence of the environment, such as long spines in quiet waters. Also an ecotype or ecophenotypic variation.

endemic: living in a certain geographical area, and usually originally confined to that region.

fathom (fm): six feet.

fauna: assemblage of animals living in a certain region. Flora refers to the plant life.

form or forma: a minor genetic

variant, colour phase, aberration, or variation due to diet or environment.

fusiform: in the shape of a spindle; elongated and tapering at both ends.

gastropod: member of the class Gastropoda, as a snail, whelk, conch, periwinkle, volute etc.

genus: a group of species seemingly closely related.

gerontic form: an oversized or worn condition due, in part, to old age.

growth lines: marks or flaws in the shell due to varying rates of growth or to changing environmental conditions.

habitat: the place where a species or individual customarily lives.

hermaphrodite: an individual having the organs of both sexes, as in all pulmonate and opisthobranch snails and some bivalves.

hinge: the upper thickened edge of the valve of a bivalve, usually with interlocking teeth and a ligament providing a hinge effect.

holotype: the specimen used in the description of a new species and selected to represent the species. The remaining specimens are paratypes.

hybrid: offspring coming from the parents of two different populations, usually different species.

intertidal zone: seaside zone between high and low tide marks.

lunule: a heart shaped impression in front of bivalve beaks, one half being on each valve.

malacology: study of molluscs, especially the soft parts.

mantle: a skin cape that creates the shell in molluscs.

melanistic form: black or nearly black colour form of a species.

monograph: an advanced and comprehensive treatment of a family or a group of species or genera.

morphology: the structure or form of a shell which may vary within a single species.

ontogeny: study of the growth stages and development of an individual.

osmosis: the water removing process which in the case of molluscs, occurs during the formation of a new compound from two separately composed liquids of differing concentrations. It occurs when new shell is formed at the mantle when the mantle mucus encounters existing shell layers.

operculum: a horny or shelly "trapdoor" found in some gastropods, sometimes used to close the aperture of the shell.

papilla: (plural: papillae) small projections of tissue forming minute nodes or bumps on the mantles of some molluscs such as cowries.

pelagic: living at the surface of the ocean, or customarily free-swimming in the ocean, such as *Janthina*, *Argonauta* and many squids.

periostracum: an outer, chitinous, protective layer covering the shell, sometimes smooth, rough or hairy.

phylum: a higher taxonomic group of major uniqueness, such as the starfish and sea urchins (phylum Echinodermata) or the molluscs (phylum Mollusca).

plankton: plants and animals, usually very small, that are free-swimming or floating on or near the ocean's surface.

prodisoconch: embryonic shell of a bivalve or scaphopod. In gastropods called a protoconch.

Quaternary: the most recent geological era, extending from the

Pleistocene to the Holocene, which succeeded the Tertiary period one million years ago.

radula: a tooth found on the lingual ribbon (or "tongue"). Plural: radulae. Found in all classes of molluscs except bivalves.

range: geographic area in which a species lives.

sculpture: the surface markings on a shell, such as ribs, scales, cords, etc.

sinistral: coiling counterclockwise, or "left-handed". When a sinistral gastropod is held with the apex up and the aperture towards the viewer, the aperture is on the left side.

species: a distinct, genetically isolated series of actually or potentially interbreeding populations.

subspecies: a geographical, somewhat isolated, race with minor differences.

substrate: the floor or bottom of the water, usually of sand, coral or rock.

taxonomy: the study of classification and identification.

Tertiary: geological era extending from the Palaeocene to the Pleistocene (about 60 million years duration).

type: specimen(s) used in describing a new species (see holotype and paratype).

umbilicus: the recessed area deepening to form the aperture of gastropod shells.

umbones: the raised area towards the back of each valve on a bivalve shell, placed immediately above the hinges; the upper and earliest part of the valves.

valve: one half of shell of a bivalve clam.

variety: a minor form, such as a special colour or shape, but not a subspecies.

varix (plural: *varices*): elevated, axial rib on the whorls of a snail, sometimes bladelike or frilled.

veliger: molluscan larval stage, usually free-swimming.

vernacular name: the name of a taxon in any language other than the language of zoological nomenclature. Popular or common name.

whelk: any large snail shell, usually a *Fasciolaria*, *Colus* or *Cittarium*.

whorl: a complete turn of a coiled snail shell.

Index

Some useful references

ABBOTT, R. TUCKER. American Seashells, 2nd edition. Van Nostrand/
  Reinhold, N.Y. 1974.

HUMFREY, MICHAEL. Sea Shells of the West Indies. Collins, London. 1975.

SUTTY, LESLEY. Seashell Treasures of the Caribbean. Macmillan,
  London. 1986.

WARMKE, GERMAINE and R. T. ABBOTT. Caribbean Seashells. Dover
  Publications, N.Y. 1961.

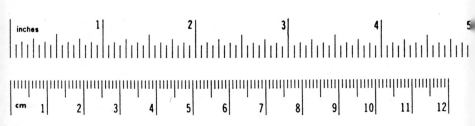